Unproclaimed Words
of a Teenage Boy

Unproclaimed Words

of a Teenage Boy

❖

Tanner Brodie Fenton Croft

To order additional copies of this book, contact:
Xlibris Corporation
1-888-795-4274
www.Xlibris.com
Orders@Xlibris.com
56029

1

Half awake, eyes squinting to the bright light, cold, tired, another morning, another day, I wake slowly, as like to a bear coming out of hibernation. I'm not a morning person—lots of people aren't, at least that's the way I see it—but I'm just a teen, no reason to listen to me. I wasn't hung over today. It was a school day; if I took the risk of showing up to classes with a hangover, there wouldn't be a point of being there headache and all. But I guess you gotta drink sometime, right? I mean, it's always fun, isn't it? Like the time you had so much to drink you got all depressed over a girl and tried to kill yourself, or how about the time when you decided to use cocaine and overdose on it and your friends, leave you in a wheelbarrow, call 911, and walk away. I mean, that's gotta be fun, right? You find out really who your friends are. It's not fun, but we do it all anyway to be popular, to impress our so called friends, we do it just to do something that weekend, have something to talk about when we get back to school. We're just a bunch of kids growing up, we got our parents on our case all the time. It's funny though 'cause they almost always act like they never drank or partied when they were our age but we all know they did. It's for them to hide that fact when you hear them bring it up with relatives at family reunions or when their close friends are over and reminiscing about the past. Who are they to judge us? Sure, sure, they care and they use that as their number one defense, "I care about you, you shouldn't drink so much." It's like some huge guilt trip from our parents, for instance, when they say they're disappointed for the first time ever and it hits you, *But why?* We're just doing what they did; life at this age is meant to be fun, isn't it?

~

Shaking, shaking, shaking, the bedsprings creaking up and down from the pressure and movement. "Get up! Get up! I called you half an hour ago and you're still lying here, you're gonna miss the bus if you keep that up." This is my mom telling me everything I already know. I'm just a know-it-all teen to everyone, you know, except this was the second time this morning she had woken me up so maybe I'm not as smart as I look. Aggggh . . . disgruntled pleasure standing to my feet with a long wailful yawn, now scavenging around my room, grabbing what I could see of my dirty laundry—yesterday's clothes, of course—just tossing them into the laundry basket on my way to the bathroom. Flick the light switch on my way into the bathroom; *Vro . . . Vro vrooo . . . nnnhnhhnh*, these are the noises of the fan that turns on with the light, always I wonder when that damn thing is going to fall out of the ceiling and hit me square in the head. My mom always and I mean always, wants me to be fast in the bathroom, always telling me to have a shower, but I like it slow so I have a bath. It takes a while, but that's perfect; it gives me time to brush my teeth and flex muscles that I don't have in the mirror. Lots of kids choose to work out in physical education, I, on the other hand, would rather do a lap of the field, great cardio, not great for my flexing muscles though. It always seemed like such a chore, ya know, up, down, up, down, up, down, always so boring then I got friends saying, "How aren't you able to work out, look at your brothers." Phh, the funny thing with that is that they make it sound like weight lifting is in my blood or something, but truth has it that my brothers were just as skinny until taking steroids and owning their own gym so in a way they're no better than me but I'm no better than them for not trying. You see, to succeed in the object before me; I haven't really failed until I really try to lift weights. I don't need muscle though—well, not the overrated type; there's no need for it unless of course I wanted to look like Arnold Schwarzenegger which I don't. Out of the bath now, running to my room, clothes all over in different stacks—black shirt, white socks, Warehouse One low-cut jeans—they're not tight emo ones though, but what if they were? Would people think I go home and cut myself 'cause of what I wear? How cynical is our conscience; this is the kind of world where fashion is the image of one's standards. Oh yes, I can't forget my blue Denver Hayes boxers, that grey hoody I always wear on those cool nights when I chose to run down to the bridge, passing a silent village that's filled with wonder. I run up to the small bridge and I stop and I glance down over to the river bed and I see constant memories of fishing with my friends then turning around as if to find my beat in my breath, looking down, placing those black Vans sneakers on my feet, my left shoe with black laces and my right with white laces, a look of security to the one wearing them, nothing to do with color of skin or a spectacle of attention they're just shoes with a boy in them. Running much faster now, I steam up from the back of the building, aka my house, to the front of the building, my parents' café "Malakwa Café." Yes yes, I know you're confused, thinking oh my god, where does he live ? Well, it's this little town or village if you will go about thirty minutes away from a bigger town called Salmon Arm; they're known for their Jewels and Gold, basketball teams wearing the school colors of yellow and blue that often ranked top 10 in the province of British Columbia. Now as I was saying, my parents Rhona Martin and Brian Croft are not married, I'm a bastard child (as some might refer me as), have a café built in and attached to our house, with a slap together open-minded setup look to it, yet very warm and bright with the recently repainted living room walls with the offset white look to it. The café, on the other hand, has a look of an old dark diner, yet you wouldn't know this feeling with the windows providing much light, making it a more open environment to enjoy your meals and, of course, your coffee. I yet only realized the greater look of the café with the rustic cedar walls, the room filled with my mother's teapots, her collection starting so small now; so grand amazing how that happens, isn't it? From one to hundreds in a spread of a few years, a few birthdays and Christmases. Now out I come, backpack on my left shoulder, lunch made in my hand, the look of beginning of the day, the one you see in movies the "have a good day at school" moment so little yet in films as a character's first day of school, so what's the brilliance of it all. I can still remember my first day. It was a big deal; my grandma Isabel walked me across the road and we waited. I still have that photo around somewhere; now however I don't walk across the road due to reinforced rules of the school district and now the driver waves us on rather than us as passengers just stepping aboard feeling our own security rather than a driver's decision to put us on at their accord. Ready now, I strap that very dependable black-and-blue backpack on my shoulder again, it's lasted a while now, four years I guess with two Europe trips, now those were fun, that was the first time I was ever really truly drank and those were some great memories to be had. All ready and set, a yellow bus seen, my bus to ride on, I know now it's time to go. Waiting out in the cold only a moment, then she pulls up, lights flashing, stop sign popping out the side, then finally her signal to come aboard. "Good morning," says Kathy in her usual format, this the words of our bus driver, the one that drives oh so slow yet always looks out for us while doing so, I mean, if she didn't take the time to drive slow and pay attention to the road, I could be saying this from a grave, except I don't want to be buried I want to be burned and turned to ashes, this way I'll be spread all over the world and I'll enjoy it, God, I'll enjoy it even if I am dead 'cause we died on the school bus but really we didn't, we have a good bus driver, a veteran bus driver in the sense of experience, not age or level. Scrambling now to find a seat, I finally found a seat, it's near the midsection of the bus, seat 11 I think it was, sitting here now I make myself comfortable, knees raised digging into the seat, it's always better if there's a fat kid sitting in front of you. That way their weight holds your knees in place and there's much more comfort over a skinny lightweight because with the skinny kid, your knees are always falling and it's a pain in the ass when that happens. Opening my backpack now, I reach in and pull out my tangled, knotted headphones and my iPod, placing one in each ear, starting the music on a lower volume then setting off to high volume so I don't have to listen to everyone's stories and problems on the bus it's just so annoying, people's problems, that is. I can be left alone in my own world. The slow, yet safe drive now begins, straight up to the STOP sign about one hundred meters away then taking a left then a right onto the TransCanada Highway 1, now straight on out, passing a mill and houses then the last campground on that stretch the KOA campground; I worked there you know. That was my first job; I cleaned the pool there every morning over the summer, it only took two hours, but it was worth it. For some reason, it was enjoyable; I don't know why though. The owner then was my friends' parents' hosts if you will, at least that's what the KOA corporation rather prefer they call themselves. I however, knew them simply as Maurice and Donna Lepage, very nice people, no longer owners there now though. Maurice sold the campground to his brother. I golfed with his brother; well, his other brother Wilfred, the one that took it over, was Donald I think. I don't know, I don't go around there anymore, probably better off anyway. *Bump bump!* Always so annoying those potholes, well, there's lots of them I hate; it's a minefield of potholes going from Malakwa to Sicamous. Now Sicamous, that's a small town, is not considered a village this time, mainly because it has a much higher population than Malakwa. Sicamous is actually known for something, well, so is Malakwa, but weed is illegal so that doesn't count. It used to have its mill though, its big mill, that is; it employed a lot of people in both Malakwa and Sicamous until they shut it and laid a lot of workers off, that is. The secretary that is at my school worked there for years in the Office. Now then the "Houseboat

Capital of Canada", that's what Sicamous is labeled as, or that's what they're proud of, I don't see why, I mean—WOW!! A big trailer with pontoons on the water, that's a real achievement, eh gawd, now I'm really rolling my eyes, why couldn't they just keep money out of town pride. Now and then "town pride" is only one thing in Sicamous that's better than the beach and that's our hockey, already having two players in the NHL with action and more draft picks waiting for game time. Then there's the Sicamous Eagles Junior B hockey club, a once great powerhouse hockey club now an embarrassment to league standings, picking players short of raw talent, giving up home boys for players from Kelowna who have half the talent and half the heart, picking a team that can't play the game well, playing for the name on the back, not the name on the front of the jersey. It's sad really that the young kids all around come here and have them to look up to them. Management must not know that we want a winning team; they must not know that we want a group of hometown boys gracing our ice. It's an embarrassment to the town when they bring in others to try and put up a winning team that appears to suck ass. That's no disrespect to the players before them because they were champions unlike our dysfunctional team to date. When will the tide turn? When will ignorance not blind power? Why would Sicamous people go to a hockey game not knowing anyone on it? When will the little guy try out for the team and make it? Politics, that's what it is. When will a hometown bear and breed a hero, put on an eagle uniform, and score the game, winning the goal just to prove a point? Skill exceeds, but heart is what gives you greatness, something our players lack. There is that fact that they come from far and wide and they come to our school, the overlooked eagles player the look of a jock chewing every day rarely in class and we have girls here that love them, the pucks, but of course wasting every second of every minute trying to get in bed with them, the prettiest of girls throwing themselves away for nothing but a lie, what are these girls thinking, just to make them feel special. Each of the guys has a girl waiting back home, oh the trickery, the life of a puck. These are my opinions on our hockey club, but I know others think the same. I just remember a time when I was much younger and that same team, that same logo was feared by other teams in the league, what happened to pride in all this. After all, it's more than just a sport, it's supposed to be a player's way of life, and it shows that their way of life is dead when they're not winning or even being considered for the team.

Unproclaimed Words of a Teenage Boy

~

We pass so many campgrounds on this ride to school, if only we could pause and stand still with tents and campfires all being one; this statement of one is unjust in this world and our school, why do we choose hate over dislike? Is it 'cause it's a shorter word, easier to say? Judgment in this futile age will override the makers of the look. I had to try and sound smart, haha, that's my way of saying that our opinion on others will rise to deformed growth and will show within our school body. Before, it was always jocks and geeks, but now it's grown to the proportion of emos, greasy kids, smokers, jocks, geeks, tough guys, fatties, pucks, eagles, preps. It's all just a lie; if we took off whatever it is that hides who we really are, we could see a better brighter world. Now Entering Sicamous, Population 3,000, Houseboat Capital of Canada—I wonder if they can really be the Houseboat Capital of Canada, probably not, but it gets the tourists which equals money within the community. *Thump, thump, thump!* Gotta love those potholes, I hope spring rolls around soon so that they, the community, can fix them. Slowing down now to sixty kilometers per hour turning left, now right, passing the Tru-Value Hardware Store and pulling off to the right to reach the destination of Eagle River Secondary, our high school. Pulling the headphones out of my ears now waiting for the call to get up. *Phzz, phzz!* "Safe to get up," all the static making it hard to hear Kathy, but we all knew it was coming, we're used to it, twelve years used to it, comforting in a way that these things never change but still just another rule to follow, another order to be pushed around to. What if we all stood up, took a stand, changed the rules? Would they allow for such involvement in the way the school system works? But then their rule on direct defiance comes into play, always over nothing; why do we as students fear those words or the person saying them, slowly coming out of our teachers' mouth? "Direct Defiance, got to the office," after all it is what we're supposed to do, what we're capable of, all we're trying to do is better ourselves in an environment fit for teacher rule. The secretary, "Ms. Rabbitt" is always nice to us. She does not look down on us but sees us as all equal. She is always kind to us and lets us vent which makes us feel better before we get the call to go into the "Big Office" where the power is exerted. We ask the questions, they answer them, that's how it works, that's how it always worked; but now it's turning to a dictatorship in the classes, almost always looked down upon or seen differently just over the wrong answer or wrong frame of word. And then you wonder why you're seen as an outcast, always judged, always shunned, this the life of a teen at one point or another in his or her life. It's funny now 'cause in English class, we're just told how to feel about a poem; there's nome of our own feelings involved, it's the teacher's answer or nothing, and what is the point, the writer of the poetry does not write for a teacher's one answer, yet for many answers. That's the joy of imagination. We all see different things, not always the same, we are all different yet all the same. Walking past I see a chocolate bar wrapper; I don't pick it up, I don't have such emotion over the well-being of our school's grass. Last week in the bus line, "keep off the grass, keep off the grass," every three minutes that's what Mr. Beeftink would say, and what is the purpose for this? To keep it looking well and proper? Why is it such a big deal to him though? I mean yes, he's worked here for over twenty years, but what satisfaction, if any, does he get from that? I won't ask; I'm sure the answer will be so long and well developed that I'll fall asleep standing up and I'm sure everything he says will be ever so precise and right as usual in his classes, that's how he is as a teacher. I always considered him to be the wisest of teachers, good for advice and knowledge. It's hard to believe this 2008 year could be his last as a teacher, sad really, he likes it so much and it's always a pleasure for students to be in his classes. I am sure he can do something else though, with less stress, but deep down it's not right you know that feeling, that itch. After all, I'm sure the school is probably as comforting as his own home after all the hours he's put in to teaching. I think I'll pick up that piece of garbage after all, save myself the guilt of hurting the environment even though I didn't drop it in the first place. Walking straight now, along the worn-out concrete path, it is wintertime after all so the weather does have an effect on concrete. There's no ice on it today, just a puddle not clear though almost mud yet still not thick enough to stick. Now reaching the second door of three entrances, a pause then a gawk then I walk in, always wiping my feet off on the green-brown carpets, now stepping to the hall you can hear other students forcing the wet squishing sound from their shoes all the way down the hall, leaving a big puddle for the custodians to clean, I'm sure. Now why would you want to do that, I mean they're nice guys always treating us as students well, saying hello when they see us and they're always cleaning up after us and sure it's their job, but we should also not be pigs and clean up after ourselves. I look left, glance down the hall, this is the hallway for grade 12s. I should probably be in that part of the hallway, but someone else got my locker. So I go right then left then right again. I now stand in front of locker 296, placed down the grade 8 hallway; the stinky grade 8 hallway I mean really, is it that hard to use some deodorant or some body wash so you smell at least half decent to the others in the school, but now I'm just being judgmental. Turn around, graduation photos on the wall, my graduation photo on the wall; this is grade 13 for me the allegations of me being a failure are very true. I never apply myself you know, I always seem to have things under control but I don't; I am normal after all. It's just the whole disappointment stage it's still falling into place, I still haven't felt the feelings of failure but when I do, it's going to hit me hard. Not because I let my parents down, just because I let myself down, I never reached for any goals and now last year is all a bad memory filled with guilt and fear. I see more than just memories in that grad photo; I see friends, some I hardly knew at the time, but they cared; you know the ones that would always ask what you were doing on the weekend and if you went then they would get you involved in their plans. These are the people I miss, all off working or going to college somewhere, it seems that the only time I'll see them again is in the mall one day when we're all a couple years older and will ask how things are as if we were much older, but didn't; we just graduate I'll tell myself as if I graduated with them. You see, I don't exactly like adopting change in my life; many people don't. That's probably why I came back trying to keep my feeling of youth in tacked, it's not easy growing up yea know all the drama and depression all the stages of change even lead some people to suicide. Oh no—8:23 a.m.; I hope there's still at least one blueberry bagel left in the cafeteria, straight then to the right through our gym doors take a right downstairs and bingo! Food! "Well good morning, Mr. Tanner, did you watch *One Tree Hill* last night?" "Yea I did, it was okay. Nathan better get rid of that babysitter though. Yea, I'll get the blueberry one and cream cheese, please." This all coming from Adam's mom Shannon; she's a nice lady always giving us good healthy grub down in the cafeteria, this also being forced on by the uprising rate of obesity in our country, it's sickening knowing that people are helpless to move only because they can't make the time to exercise and eat right; just poor costly habits I guess. Adam is, well, my friend, ex-teammate in basketball and he helps me write songs; he graduated last year with my past. "Your bagels ready." "Thanks, I'll see ya later." Back up the stairs and to the bleachers in the gym, sitting now somewhat awake and chilled by the cool gym look. Over the past two years I have used up my life sitting or playing in this gym. The room that I value most in the school; so bare but great, we don't need all the banners like most schools to enjoy what we have. There are no cuts in our school teams, everyone getting a chance to play, no matter their condition or skill level, this shows character in our school teams, we might not have a bunch of skilled players but we have fun and we have good memories. *Click, bam!* Door slams shut, now 8:35 a.m., no one's here might as well try and write a song again. Over this past year, I've found myself with good rhyming and wording scheme when it came to songs. So I've been writing all these lyrics as a way to escape my real emotions on the world and my life, It's not some diligent excuse of counselor feeling crap, it's art, it's my form of wording how I feel about everyone and everything, read this for example it's one of the better ones.

Driving to Dead

Beautiful girl come ride with me
my car is slow just like the moments we have
we'll get these feelings when we touch
all of this is not enough

first date drama, but where to begin
kiss me now and in an hour or so again
hold back on tears old memories just make you cry
smile once and then just die in my arms
Just hurry now and don't be shy
We're gonna be late, it's the last chance to dine
It's the last chance to dine

don't know what to do
my feelings they were meant to be with you
And now we're on our own
trapped inside this world
who are we now

last looks, and you accident prone
kiss me now and in an hour or so again
hold back on tears old memories just make you cry
smile once and then just die in my arms

Just hurry now and don't be shy
We're gonna be late, It's the last chance to dine
It's the last chance to dine.

It's death, it's love, it's that feeling that you know who you're forever is with and for that one moment you're the most alive. I write all these songs and then I get this feeling that what if they're good enough to be good songs, and I pace and I pray that they are. If I could live a musician's life, I would; but if I couldn't, I'd make damn sure that people knew who wrote those songs. "Hey, Unky Tanny." I didn't catch who said it, but it was friendly, a friendly hello. Now what if I didn't know the person yet they still say it's oh so cuttle, and why do they do this? For attention or just the importance of saying hello; sure, it's friendly but what made hello so popular to the unknowns? I am an uncle, that is the first context of the name I was just called. I've been an uncle since I was two; I have fifteen nieces and nephews to date. Annoying, fun, all still learning important values in life; this the way it should be, the learning stage if you will, finding responsibility, whether it's mowing the lawn or helping dad fix the bobcat or maybe it's taking care of your siblings while Mom and Dad are away. All new aspects in a preteen era in a person's life. Although emotions are higher and greed is well-known with jealousy and at her age you wouldn't think that a little girl could call 911, well, my niece did and I was babysitting and she called 911 because I wouldn't say "I love you" as an uncle. Such bullshit. Where do all these immature reactions come from? I blame television, a teacher or politician would say when really all it was, was her brother and sister. All speculation over so little truth. *Beeeep!* Time to start A block.

2

C lustered mind now setting in, the void between reality and fantasy now filling in the holes of my thoughts. Out of the gym now straight down the hall I came, walking steadily but not fast, no, not fast, who walks fast to get to class, could you imagine what people would think if I walked fast to get to class. All probably unjustly assuming I was in love with classes and learning, a nerd per se is what they would think of me. So I stop for a drink, not long though, so many people in line for water today; if I took my time they would think I was better than them or maybe that I can't afford water where I come from as my friends like to joke with me about, them being from Sicamous and I from Malakwa always giving each other little joke to remind us as to where we come from. I don't mind the fact that they do that; it's just what security does that give them when they're trying to win an argument. We only live ten minutes apart, what's the big deal to them, sure, they have a better outcome on the look of their community with all the stores and shops but who ever said we needed it? I mean, I enjoy my privacy, I enjoy the fact that I can go around and drink with my friends and not have the cops all over the place watching our every move. I like the comfort that we all know each other. We can all say hello, and we have just enough land in our property that we have privacy from our neighbors. This is unlike the devouring heart of the Sicamous infastructure with their big-rise buildings on the beaches and their kitty corner houses, giving the word *private* the notion that your neighbor might not hear you talking about him through your paper walls. Prices rising, houses selling condos going up, the cheap duplex a simple reminder that land can be valued more than people think; childhood in a small town much better than a city, the word-finding clarity while growing, childhood, childhood, whispered in your mind, that soft memory of forbidden times that kept you going as a child, one with energy and adventure, building tree houses, finding your first crush, and dreaming to be someone big when you've aged.

~

Now and then on your way, getting to class just not fast, stepping along ever so carefully, pacing my walk with the row of lights above, watching each clock tick as I walk past the old-school grad portraits, seeing familiar faces of my now present, relinquished as its own. Taking a left at Room 17, one deep breath then one in, taking my back-row seat, waiting for the others to be filled but they won't be; there hasn't been a big population here at Eagle River Secondary in quite sometime, with grad-class numbers dwindling away, who's to say we won't be shipped off to Salmon Arm for better classes. This, of course, a frantic outburst of me being absurd to the point of insanity; the point is it could happen one day if the only families coming in are summer tourists from Alberta with a time-share for a few weeks. I mean, what do we need to do to raise the population in this small town, put in a Wal-Mart? I'm sure that would go over well destroying another small town's small businesses. So tell me, if we know that the corporation hurts our towns, then why do we allow it to happen? More money in the wallet, what a shame, a fraud to the little guy under the thumb of the high-end moneymaker politician that allows for all these Wal-Marts coming in. "Now then, how's everyone today? You happy to be here learning math (pause) oh come on, that was supposed to be a joke, man. You guys are a hard bunch of kids to make laugh." This is my block A, Math 10 teacher; it's his first year here and already making a positive impact by introducing the sport of wrestling to the students here. Our team doing very well under his vision and learning paths to the sport, having four or so players on the team eligible to go to the provincials, this is a great accomplishment in the span of only a few months of teachings. I remember on the first day how he told us that he does everything very fast and is forgetful of things, sometimes spelling his name backward or incorrectly it all leads you to wonder what's going on in people's lives; does he have a medical problem? Is that it, or is it just as simple as memory loss just even for a moment or two? This is all fine; it's a natural way to hide what's going on, not meaning my teacher now, but others. The ones with the secret that you can't quite make out this person being your friend and when they finally tell you what their secret was, they're dead with the secret. They never got to tell you because they were rushed to the hospital that day, placed in the ER, and later passed away leaving you with an empty phone call and their last words all on your mind. A meaning of tragedy in the world around us. I remember going to the hospital in Salmon Arm, here seeing my grandmother aged with a stroke and cancer, a chilling feeling seeing the ones we love in dire need of help and we cannot help but waste our awaiting move with those transitional words that redeem helpless with the shadows of death. It's natural, I know, but it's painful, that burden of knowing they're gone and not able to be seen until in distant dreams. Turning my page to 43 as directed on the board, questions 1-8, I have questions, not the most cunning but they're valued in my frame of mind. One, when you're in that constant time of high school, why do we let those memories go with age? Two, with regret of our past, can we ever grow fond of what we had before we made that mistake? Now three, my brother Damyen told me once at work that I'll miss playing hockey; why did he say that, was it because he too threw it away after being such a great player in his time? Four, why do my joys in life often have to be related to sport, why couldn't it be about making something of doing a good job on a test, why can I see joy in the discomforting parts of my life? Five and still alive, why do I enjoy the run on a cold rainy day, passing through the small town I love, looking in greater detail at things I see every day, but now I see depth on the old car bridge and I see youth in the old school I went to, but why do I value these of so little value to others? Six, why were we given fears if only to fight them with our heart? Now seven, why am I resolved as a person when I walk on to a court and shoot three after three even when missing still finding comfort and just? My jersey number 8, why do we the underdogs strive off adversity and step up to the challenge when it comes to the greater good in life? These are my thoughts on my life, my sublime stumbling, muttering words in my head all leading to the heart. If you ever told me that my brother Damien would ever say something that thoughtful to me about a sport that he loved to play, I'd think you were crazy. I never knew what he valued, still don't, but that's a look at what maybe he left behind, something he didn't push to achieve, that chance to play what you love for the rest of your life. A shame, really, having so much potential yet throwing it away for a bargain on your dreams. My boss told me once that he picked up my brother hitchhiking and they were driving along and my boss asked him, "So what do you want to do with your life?" My brother turned and said, "Well, I'm either going to be a professional hockey player or a professional pitcher." What happened to that kid? The one with the dream? Was he just overrun with easy money, the easy way out? I think so. I wish I could have that image of what he was and show it to who he is, maybe he would feel something for his regrets then, maybe his old figure of a lost teen would show up. I was never so great to be placed on a good hockey team or to have a ball in my hand and say, "Strike him out!" That just wasn't me, it was him though, his past. "Tanner, are you understanding these questions?" My asking this to every student that he passed, all of us giving the simple nod of gesture that we get it and understand the meaning of the simple algebra questions from the text. Really though, I see it as a firm way of telling our teacher that we don't wish for him to stand over us; that sharp awkward feeling as though he's insulting our intelligence, what if the students stood over the teacher in awe, would they to feel the blister of uncertain ease scorched through the eyes in the back of their head? Who are they watching now? Twiddling my pencil in uncertain thoughts, here my imagination slips away, walls of the room fall, my train of thought gone staring into the abyss. Thinking of how to get away, always finding this place holds me back to certain extents that I no longer can explain. I'm afraid to leave this town, always the dark thought, just a picture of a boy beside the sign saying Now Leaving Home, but where does leaving take me—to a future dead or living, or to the unknown girl I await in my dreams? Insecure, lost, cracking flaws, all fears when I leave home, what interest is this to my falling demise? Gasping for breath in a water-filled room, what depth is greatness in a drowning cause? Reaching for all these great heights that only mean something to you, justified with negative outlooks from others whose wishes don't comprehend your path to greater living. With these obstacles, we cannot strive on living and rising up, yet we strive off our opposite negative energy, always stepping up to prove them wrong, the props wielding our fire. Papers passed back with a notion to study these notes for our test tomorrow, I won't study though, too many distractions, my mind doesn't comprehend the knowledge to the word *study* nor does it seek to exist. I've always wondered what my outcome would be if I took brain-enhancer drugs for focus in the classrooms, probably just make me more depressed if anything. I drink Red Bull though, often four cans or so a day, most people thinking I just drink it for a long day high, this, however, false to my own conception, finding that it wakes me for my classes and work yet makes me weaker, I'm sure, in the long run, just throwing my money away on a fool's gold. What to comprehend in school? The good and the bad of life, poverty and rich, learning that only brains will get you somewhere in life, this probably what the geeky nerd kids would tell you like one of my friends, for example, always thinking that I'm stupid, jabbering me with his jokes. I don't think he knows how it affects me but it does; I want a life, you see. He can have his marks and his doctor's job, but that's not happiness, that's greed of something you don't want nor need. I realize now people of his kind are ignorant when they think themselves better than all of us. There's a teacher here and her values of learning are oh so much more important than what we as students see, valuing only the smartest of the boys and the rest of the girls, mainly sexist to the weaker sex of learning. I remember times when I did an image and to her it was all wrong, it had to be because she herself didn't like it as if her voice matter in the art form of the school. What gives her the right to judge one's art with such prestigious principles that sets us all off if misconformed gestures, making us all feel weak and unaware that what we make is good? We should not hide what we are because of one judgmental person's attribute to attack the weaker few. Even choosing to badger me for coming back to learn and upgrade my knowledge, making me the point of laughter in the class, sure later apologizing but what right has she when I simply sat there all in class doing my work and lashing to me over other students' miscondoned humor toward the teacher, causing her in an uproar of some noble pride over nothing. I'm a pawn in the school this year, always being informed and blackmailed by teachers that this is my thirteenth year and they can have me removed, but what emotionless sense do they get when they imply this? I don't understand; I thought this year was supposed to be positively a chance for me to change the past. Maybe I was wrong with such negative sublimation from those in power, from those the ones who are supposed to encourage me yet do not. "Here you go and good job by the way maybe I was wrong about you in this class after all," this a test, the first one this year, that I got 80 percent. That's not the point though; the point is the week during the writing of this test I was at home with the flu unable to write it, so without any marks in, my teacher has presumed that I'm stupid and don't get it. It's all okay though; I stepped up, I proved him wrong, that's the point. If you can rise to the challenge and do well, it's worth it seeing the look on the face of ignorance, in fact I encourage all of you to do the same, step up, my brother did. Not the hockey player but the one that was addicted to drugs, some days he wouldn't come home to his family of four kids and one being a newborn baby; it's not easy, he made the right choice, thought family over drugs. I was happy when I heard that he did that, he's a hard worker and one of the most down-to-earth people you will ever know of and now after rising up and getting rid of the drugs, he's able to make ends meet. Ten minutes left in class now, all our books closing up, classmates getting ready to go to the next block in the rotation. The walls now coming back into perspective, the boundaries of this life here for the next four months, sure we can go out and party, but if we do something wrong, they'll hear about it and when we come back, we'll get a lecture, a slap on the wrist, or maybe a phone call home—this is the system of a running community. Sure, not all the teachers know us, but garmented one will and they'll pass judgment and opinion on the subject and then you'll go home and deal with it, the boundaries are everywhere until we're out, until school's out for good. Waiting still, I pull out my iPod and headphones, I look for a soothing song, one that relaxes the mind and makes me feel at will with where I am for the day. I remember now why I see my brother Damien as a person doesn't value me in his life, at least that's what I thought when I was eight; I was adventurous at this age, as most kids are. I was out poking the ice on the pond with a stick and kept on reaching for more ice when I fell in; I couldn't swim then and still can't to this day but I was scared, I was splashing arms, flailing in and out, in and out, screaming for help I was certain I was a goner. Someone heard me though, not my brother, my friend David; he was up in my tree fort adding his own unique something to it. He jumped from the high treetop, came running over, and pulled me out. Minutes later, I would appear in the house in front of a young teen, me soaked, and all he could say was, "Get outta the way, Tom Green's coming on." I just almost died and that's all he could fathom to say; he didn't even ask why I was soaked as if it were an everyday look he kept watching the TV. I don't think he's ever been compelled to want to get to know me, always so distant, never wanting to be in my life but yet when he takes me golfing for the first time, it's as if he thinks he's always been there as big brother yet instead he took off and chose a path that changed his life forever. I now won't buy into his fake glamour of drug money; as a child, sure, this because I didn't know any better but because if it ever mattered, I wish he was around, not because he then would have picked a different path but for the memories even if only a few. These are past views that can't matter now; it's time to see what I had, not what I didn't have. I had friends always looking out for me, all still doing so today. When you can get used to the lost time and framed pictures without those people in them, you can be someone, you can be yourself. I've always felt like I was following some stupid shadow of his by playing hockey and baseball, but I wasn't. I was learning to love sports as a young child, this giving me new levels of skill which I now can use in the many things I do in my life. Rambling on, sitting in a desk talking to myself in my head, am I crazy? *Beep!* Finally, off to geography, slipping out of my desk, out the door I came, turning left to locker 296, grasping the cool metal lock, putting the numbers 21, 59, 21, *click*, now in my locker, I trade off math binders for geography binders, *slam! Click*, locked up. Going straight to the left then left and right down the hallway before reaching the wheelchair ramp then turning right and finding my seat in the top left side of the class, throwing my books down, walking out now heading back toward the gym, getting that drink I've longed for all day. Passing a young teen Brandon Scott, I notion a high five hand and as well as say hello, he say hey and gives me an enthusiastic high five with a smile. Brandon's a nice kid but is mentally challenged; it's sad but he plays such an important role in our school, greeting everyone with an open door, saying hello, he's not afraid to be here and that's great to know. I just wish he could participate in much more like everyone else; we try to get him involved in lots of things, but is it enough? I wish he could have more. This shows that life isn't always fair, but we need to make the best of it. Walking farther now, I pass my past, always pausing as if to greet an old friend in that photo, will these feelings of regret haunt me for the years to come, or is this just a wake-up call for my future's day?

3

An entrance glows, the sun shining in from the courtyard window and me still in a stance of utmost attraction with the once-uprising student who had a chance to take advantage of all those dreams. The clock's not moving; it's set to the past with a pause as if going back I can still see them all around me saying hello and all laughing at stupid things that meant nothing to others but something to us, this all to our dry, sarcastic humor. I see myself always joking the first time I took English 12 and PE 12, always having attitude as if to impress the people that don't care, the ones that are not here anymore because they chose to succeed with their classes, they chose to see past the distractions, something I only wish I could do. Yet those distractions do come with a value, making classes livable and less zoned out to what is being taught, all the paper airplanes and paper balls, the laughing and terrible jokes, the simplest people seen walking on the road to hearing an ambulance go by, all making our imaginations run wild with constant highs of our energy and tired now, thrown away like the banana peel we do not choose to eat with its bitter flavor and great color of yellow, bringing the thought that we are all monkeys fighting for survival. Taking a walk now in this past life of my imagination, I see myself; I peer through the window of the gym's blue door. I'm sitting there in the center of the court; I remember this day very well, it was last year around the month of April. There was no one else here, I stayed behind after that day of classes, just sitting there in dead silence looking at all the dust beneath me on the hardwood court. I was thinking of how I screwed up, how I drove myself to a laid-back failure that wanted to graduate but wouldn't be that year. That was then though; this is now—back to time, back to present. I now have all intentions of graduation, the first of my mom's kids, I'm sure I let her down before but I intend to fix that mistake. It's something I have to do, yea know, that feeling of what's right and what's wrong, the thought of knowing I can do it if I only just apply myself. Walking now faster and more restless, the thought of being late now sinking in, *thud, thud, BAM!* On the floor now, going too fast, I guess I must have tripped over myself, maybe for a purpose though, something caught my eye down there, not a penny but a dime, an American dime at that, you got to wonder how many people all over have had this little coin in their pocket, hand even mouths just throwing it off to the side under a bench as if they don't need pocket change, this I'm referring to as the person that dropped and left it here. What were they thinking? If they get enough dimes, that will make a dollar or two, they could go get not one but two cheeseburgers from McDonald's, not the healthiest of food, I know, but I'm young, I can handle it. After thinking of just leaving that great amount of money, I think I'm going to throw it in my shoe for good luck and safekeeping. I mean, if I ever need change, I know where to look. Getting up on my feet now, wiping the dirt off my jeans and continuing on to get my yet again and overrepeated drink of water. "Get to your classes, get to your classes," the vice principal and principal in the hallway telling us, this an everyday exercise for them, making sure we're all where we need to be and I myself should start getting there now. Walking back past the photo and back to my desk with my binders, this a long block and with geography it can drag on if you let it; the key idea is not falling asleep in the class, or you may face the consequences of embarrassment without even knowing. You see, our geography teacher, Mr. Beeftink, likes to play little mind games when you're falling asleep; so when he sees that you're passing out, almost falling out of your seat, he'll start medaling with what he's saying to the rest of the class, starting out with a lower voice then slower, getting higher and higher, causing you the one he's teasing to wake and fall asleep again with the words going soft then loud, soft then loud—it's rather amusing to witness. Looking to my left, glancing at one of the maps, I look steady and embrace a spot on the map, closer and closer I look until I see where I love that sweet place of Europe. I remember back last year sitting in the biology room where we had done our math that year, and I remember myself and two friends Matt and Andrew always talking to one another making jokes about whoever and whatever we could. Well, this day we had a substitute and instead of silent reading, I chose to go to the front of the room and look at this big old tattered here-and-there map of the world and all I said was we should go here and it was western Europe. Andrew and Matt, agreeing with this, we made up rough plans for a trip over the following summer, all excited and joyful about it then shot down like a fighter pilot in World War II, the big issue as always money, so that thought pushed aside like all the rest. Sure, I've been overseas before, but that was different, that was with the school, the boundaries apply, remember. I just wanted a year overseas, exploring all it has to offer us, not the premium package of twelve days for three grand. I can't do that again; it was fun though, God, it was fun. It's trips like that you're never going to forget, the tapestry of what we'll talk about when we're old and our children put us in a home. Lights flickering, hazing on and off, a cooling chill now coming forth from the back of the room, then black. Yay, hurray, time to go home! It was a power outage, probably not for long just a little surge. I'm afraid of the dark, someone silencing the class with their words. What are our greatest fears, the suspenseful murder seen with the killer under your bed, creepy-crawly insects, maybe the feeling of aging, showing weakness in what we used to love. I know my fear; my deepest fear is what's waiting for me after death. Some say they saw the light when they were out of commission, but it makes you wonder. Do we just sit there in blackness waiting in eternity for something that will never come, leaving our body behind yet letting our soul remain contained as an everlasting ghost which knows no boundaries yet cannot move from where it lies? There is death; that is a fact of life that we must all face, but then there is rebirth—the joys of the world, the joys of the future held in the little ones' hands.

There's an entrancing silence when the power's out, you're able to hear everything, the calmness comforting your soul, yet telling others what you say to the unknown. Just a teen, but I take value in these moments, the chance to talk and just listen to the echo of the silence within the world now shut off. The wind now tapping softly on the window, wanting in but held in contempt the weight of which is not able to shatter glass as if to shatter and show us our flaw, our cracks in our identity. No other can tell me my flaws; that is for me to see myself. They can have opinion and judgment, but something lurks over the top of this juncture, this readiness of what's waiting day by day, a lunge, a fall, a breakup, something seen by all around. This is when you realize you're a flaw, a crack in the human look. This is no negative feeling; it's a plus, it's different, it gives you that drive to be someone, one great, one independent, and one just keeping their inner soul, their childhood, their smile showing their laughter, not a flaw. There is no flaw; it's just a thought to put you down. I have my own look; no one can ever take that away, we all change day by day showing our side's light to grey. That's what I love about people; we can all be looked up to, stared upon, but we make it happen deep down. We stare back and we fight the fear to be who we were born to be. Greatness makes up people, failure makes them better; if they can fall and strive to get back up, they can grow to be greater than what they were. Confidence is something I lack, that drive to grow is something I lack, but it will come. I know it will; it all just takes time. When I walk down the halls of this school, I see people capable to grow. I see people great already; they will all get better. Just take a walk; you will see youth now staring in their eyes their fear, but down there is something waiting to change the world. That's why we're all here, isn't it? To change the world around us. I know this girl, she's bright and funny, she's beautiful and has so much potential for so much more. She's often cut down by friends, calling her stupid as if it were true; it's not though. If only you could stare into Shawna Collie's deep blue eyes, you would see a world with a beach with a sun and much positive energy; she helps me put things better into perspective, she's short and small but could carry the weight of the world on her shoulders. I believe that I really do; her laughter, it could bring something to all of us, it's just greatness in one, a good friend she is. If you ever get the chance, look into those eyes and you'll see a world of happiness. Sitting there, the darkness overpowering the class to sit in silence, hearing other students running around the halls laughing, if you could just close your eyes here, you would be happy, listening to the just wonder of young teens at their best. "So what shall we do?" Mr. Beeftink asking the class. A girl in the back asked if we could just enjoy the moment while it lasted; we all agreed with laughter, later settling like a sweet drop of rain on a lake mustered by the silence of a lakeshore breeze. Waiting now like my fear, a few minutes already feeling like eternity, I won't die here. I guess it's just that clammy feeling grasping me a look of what's ahead, a foreshadow of death in my thoughts. "Hey, dude, look at this, hahahaha," this my friend Chris showing me a picture of a lady soaking in some bathtub with clothes on, drinking beer as if to cool off. I laugh and then I look closer, and after capturing the background image, it isn't funny, it's not funny at all. You see, that lady was in the bathtub 'cause that's all she has now after a class 3 tornado flew down and caused much devastation. I don't know why we were laughing, but that's all we do, not yet feeling what it's like since we don't get huge storms like that here in the Thompson Okanagan. Chris, well, Crazy Chris as I sometimes call him, write on his binder as that, laughing at tons of stuff. He has great ambitions and quirky jokes that we often laugh at in class; he has so many ideas, just doesn't really strive on them, but he will,

I'll make sure of that. He's got talent, maybe not the best, but I see it. He likes being behind the camera, not on the spot; he's the guy behind the scene keeping us all in a comedy relief feeling, it's great and aspiring to see. It's nice to know that you have friends like him in the world right there just waiting to be great. A flash of light, power on again, the waiting in an uncertain fear, waking like out of a dream, sitting in class now blinking lots and rubbing my eyes as if to awake. "Well, that was a good day of geography," Mr. Beeftink saying in utmost sarcasm as the class laughed with him. We all just closed our books and chatted with others for the next while. What a distraction, the power going off like that, giving us time to embrace something rare, the silence in school, often not happening but it lets us think with brief noises reflecting words of curiosity and joy, this only because the power is out though, it's not an expression of understanding, it's just an immature way of being a teen. What drives us? What gives us the motivation to strive off being happy and doing stupid, immature things like setting up trash cans and running hurdles in the hall, where do we get it from? The active heart of a teen, desirable to many. I think our youth is something we take for granted; the fast-healing, healthy bodies of the future predecessors of our parents, we don't realize that if we don't take care of what we have, we'll get all beat up and bruised, causing a future of broken people. *Beep!* "Good afternoon, are you for your lunch announcements?" Everyone wishing to be on their way already, so impatient having to stay seated while we listen to something we can't hear anyway due to all the noise in the class. Off we go though, time for lunch, most kids either heading down to the cafeteria or across the street to get a slice of pizza, some even go to the local grocery store called Askew's. I work there, I'm a stock boy, putting groceries on the shelves, facing them all to look picture-perfect; there's good owners/managers there. Ron and Ardice Daniels, being husband and wife owning the store, I've known them since I was just little and they went to my brother Damien's hockey games; their son played hockey with my brother. I've often wondered if that's how I got on there because their family knows mine. I hope not; I'd feel like dirt if that were true, nice people though. They treat us well as employees, something some other places don't know how to do. Ron, a businessman, been in this grocery business quite sometime now, we often question if he ever leaves the store, always wanting everything to be perfect as a good boss would want, then there's Ardice and she thinks she's funny, always bugging the stock boys. Well, I guess we really bug her too, but that's not the point, well, there really isn't a point, but she is nice, makes sure we're all doing well and if you're nice to her she can give you days off, haha. Then there's second in command, Mr. Wayner, he's the assistant manager; he has been doing this grocery theme for quite a while as well now. He has all these funny stories of my brothers when they all used to party together and he has this image of my brother Jay that he always does it, basically involving Wayne pretending to smoke a doobie and just imitate my brother, but I gotta say it's pretty good. Yea, it's a good place to work; it's like my summer family and summer home, good times there. "Hey, Tannah! You wanna go play some basketball in the gym?" "Yea sure, just let me get my shorts and lunch." That's my friend Brian; he's over here from Korea, he's a pretty nice guy, funny as hell, he used to board with one of the teachers, but now that his mom came down, he's been living with her in a condo. He's managed to fit in very well after coming over two years ago. It probably wasn't easy when he first got here with the change in language and food and everything really. Just this year, he's been really into playing basketball so I helped him out a bit, gave him a few pointers; he's pretty good at it and people say he sucks, but he doesn't. He just never really had a chance to play and he was too late to play on the team, but I guess that's okay sometimes 'cause some people just aren't ready for that atmosphere. I'm glad I got to know him as a friend though; he's pretty good for laughter and just being there for someone to talk to, I guess. To my locker I go, pop it open, grab my shoes and shorts and my T-shirt, then I reach to the top and grab my plastic bag; in the bag is my lunch. "Hey, Brian, let's go to the bleachers," him already hoarding down one hotdog of two and mixing that with his chocolate milk, replying back with a full mouth, "Okay, let's go." Off we went walking up to the bleacher, third row of seating just past the stairs. I start eating, and Chris and Scott come along and join us. Scott is a highly energetic guy, very athletic; he's a soccer player, pretty good at it so I hear. He also plays most school sports and also is in Rescue which is pretty cool. He's a pretty good friend too; it was pretty much just him and I actually drinking on my birthday. Scott's a pretty roundabout person if I really think about it. He is always there, it's nice to know. This is pretty much the group of people I've spent first and second semesters around along with a lot of others, but when I'm playing in the gym, it's usually with those three young teenage boys, all different yet all alike. We all treat each other well, all pretty close as if brothers in a way. "Well, that was a good lunch," I say, throwing my crusts and banana peel away, along with the plastic bag. "You boys ready to play some basketball?" "Yea, why not, let's go." None of them really have that much playing experience; they just play for fun. They were not on the senior basketball team like me. Our team looked so promising at the beginning of the year, getting Cam McConnell back as point guard since he came back for half the year; this was my second year of playing shooting guard. We started seasons 1-2 then later halfway through the season, we lost to Vernon Christian, a team we should have beaten. This would be a dreadful loss because after the game, Cam went back to Golden, leaving me as point guard and captain for the North Zone playoffs. Our first game, we got beaten up pretty bad; this was expected, but I was playing terrible and just way under the weather after getting over the flu. The second game was different. In the locker room, I said one word; the word was *adversity*. This was and always will be my most memorable game, maybe because it was my last or maybe because we played with heart. The opposition, Vernon Christian, came out pretty fast and got the first basket, but we came back and got six in a row with Steller all-around defense. I came out on fire in the first half; well, for me it was good. The second half was a different story, however; Vernon came out with so much energy, our only point getters in the second half were Alex and Gaven. It was fun though; I'm just always going to have regret though, being sick, not playing 100 percent. I let my team down big-time; it was my fault we lost. My defense was terrible, and it hurt losing my last game. I love the game, but the lesson that was learned is that if we can go out, play hard, lose, and keep our heads up then we are someone, that loss will shape us forevermore. It was a big deal to me; sport is a big deal to me. If it's not winning, it's nothing, isn't that how we're supposed to play? No, this is high school, and in a little school where we all get a chance to be someone, it's all for fun and that's how it should be. Out of the change room, we come now—Scott, Chris, Brian, and I. We just check ball and play, it's fun, so many laughs, there's no pressure playing for your friends; there is or should be however when playing for a school. You're supposed to have pride wearing a jersey, you're supposed to be lucky to play the game, and you're supposed to love every second you're on the court, and I do, God, I do, hour after hour, day after day I spend just shooting. I miss it; that's not all I'll miss, but that's a lot of it. That one big room where I love to compete every day, it's a great feeling. On my very first date I played basketball, well, first I got drunk while my best friend Mitch drove for our double date, me just sitting in the passenger seat drinking home brew, really sick but it did the trick. I only did it 'cause I was so nervous and I didn't want to screw up, ya know. Well anyway, I remember we go to Salmon Arm and go to McDonald's to eat and I go to order and the guy's name is Kermit like Kermit the Frog and I was laughing so hard I almost dropped all the food. Good times, then we met the girls at the movies and, wow, I was buzzing good when I got there. I was all sweaty and scared and the movie was sketching me out buzzing and all. Well anyway, later on after that, we just went and played basketball with them and it was so fun. That's when I was still starting and, well, she was a Senior Jewel for Salmon Arm so I had to try and look somewhat good at ball; it's just that's kind of why I started playing, and now I just love the game. It's amazing how fate happens, isn't it? One ball, one bucket, one person, that's all it takes to have passion for a game and it's great.

4

Crossing the ball between my legs, stepping back and shooting the corner three ball, arm extended above my head after the ball is released, *swish!* One of the best sounds in the world, the perfect shot, making the perfect sound. Brian, giving me a high five with the calm words of "Woah, nice shot, Tanner," I check the ball to Chris and we all continue to play. This court is nothing like my home court in Malakwa, the one that my friends and I play on when we need something to do, taking up a cooler of beer and shooting around, playing a few games here and there keeping in shape over the summer; it's all for fun out there, always. On my late-night jogs, I often find myself stopping there, not just to think about the game, but to think also about my life. Talking to myself, figuring things out, it's where I find the time to judge myself, where I find peace with the world around me. It just makes me feel refreshed, stopping where I used to go to school when I was just a little lad. This is where I glance ahead, a place of stability and meaning, I always say "what if" when I'm at this court, thoughts of possibly trying out for college volleyball now long gone but I don't think I was capable; I don't think I would have been good enough. I see past those thoughts and think of what's really important—family, friends, and having fun—how we would give up so much just to see someone we love do something great, all worth it as you see their joy, their smile, their love for something. Time is not wasted for me; time is memory of what I once was. We all change, we all mature to some extent, and we value this world for what it's worth, many times taking what we have for granted. We should take our skills and we should all be someone more, someone guaranteed for success whether that be large or small, it is always something to value. Having a quick water break, we stop and relax as if for a moment, letting our sweat cool us down, breathing deep yet living in the moment of youth. In basketball, over four years of it, I've been searching for that perfect shot; sometimes I find it, sometimes I don't. I love the challenge, the growing pain to face greater odds and to defeat them all with intentions of building up a greater prominence, one that is brave in any given situation, one that will seize the day in all glory to steal readiness from a greater threat to your heart's desires, push to strive, dig deeper than the ones around you. We are all created equal; we just need to see it that way. I have these pictures of myself in games of sport, some that my dad gave me; I often would zoom in to that elapsed focus of my eyes during that time and I see no fear, just a battered heart in losing 'cause playing and working to amendable proportions. I remember just recently; I did not value who I was and what I had. I was scared of my future's palate; I have always valued my sports over my school. One night I saw this and I put it all away, I tore it all down, I ripped it off the wall, those pictures, those awards I had felt betrayed by my own inner self, this weakness that pushed me to the depth of lesser power on my soul, on my heart. "Next basket wins," those words grasped my adrenaline and I pull everything when I have that ball in my hands, going left then right, passing off to Brian, then Brian diving under the hoop and passing it back out to me, no check, no lurking presence, just time waiting for the right feeling then it comes. I step in and shoot the ball, the perfect arc, drilling the threads of the basket, making another swish and a win. No arms raised, no great joy, or valiant scream to say I won, there's no need, we're all just friends playing a simple game at lunch. I remember playing with cocky players, so rude, so fake, flawed from every second they put the ball down, from every word they say to you, they can think that they're great but they are truly far from it. I feel bad if we have tryouts in our school, not for the ones that are bad but just for one individual, his name is Russell, he has a form of muscle disease, sure he's not the best at sports but he plays with heart, always. Few people ever see this; they just think he's some spoiler of a player, but he's not and whomever says that doesn't see him diving all over the volleyball court to return a ball, something that our team has always seemed to lack, that feeling deep down that you won't give up, you won't let that ball touch the ground, and if we all had half the heart and determination that he had, we would go very far. Popping out of the change room, now waiting for the bell to ring, slowly walking out of the gym as if perfect timing because the bell at this point did go off *beeeep!* Slowly heading down to my locker, opening it and jostling around books, a short, grabbing my math material and heading into room 17 for my Math 11 class. Throwing my textbook down and binder down on my back-row desk then telling our math teacher B-Shaw that I'm getting a drink, him replying simply with, "Just make it quick," yea right, make it quick, like I'm gonna do that. Walking slowly, no obstacles in my way, a clear path heading down the hall, tracing my previous steps, pushing the front door open, now standing there outside in the midst of drying sun over the valley of Shuswap, clouds soon to roll in but not just yet; I enjoy this warmth, this natural feeling radiating over my shadow. Turning and stepping back inside, I walk back to the fountain and grasp refreshment only for a moment. Turning away, I now proceed back to room 17. Back in the room, I step over to the back and grab an old *National Geographic* magazine; I throw my journal on top of that and pretend to read while I write my poetry, this period of fake reading lasting fifteen minutes, the whole school has to do it, it's supposed to help our reading ability, haha. Pencil in my hand, focused on great detail, emotion hiding away, slowly streaming out in spurts of brilliance, line after line they come, sometimes pausing, yet I finish. I name it "Didn't Care."

> Motionless in a chair
> people often sit and stare
> I am false I am dead
> dreams once had now gone to bed
> pull the plug my body it's done
> time run out lost with doubt
> this is my end
> Alone, restrained, trapped
> something once so great
> now torn by one big mistake
> one drink, now in a chair
> so fearless I didn't care.

No one will ever read these words and tell me they are great; teachers don't see these. They see a teenager's words not good enough for them, so therefore not good enough for anyone. Shut away, my words will stay in a journal, never found, maybe one day read upon by few and muttered about but never good enough to anyone. I understand I'm used to being pushed down, the greatness held below the wave of a body of people that do not grasp for one person's words alone. Our Math 11 teacher Mr. B-Shaw is judged as somewhat of a geek, enjoying sci-fi and *Star Trek* paranoias, maybe he too is grasping out to his youth, looking for stability as an adult. We students always enjoy breaking him down to a size of proportion that in turn makes us look better than he, isn't this right?

His face often turning red over his somewhat questionable lifestyle to students, but so what, he is after all human like the rest of us. What do we see, what makes us attack his weakness? "Okay, go put your books away." I get out of my seat and stare outside, out a window, a fragrance in the midst as if rain were to fall from the sky; it didn't though. Grass patches now coming to be seen as the once-bright sun melted the white snow flooring of the front pathway. I opened my textbook, peered at the passed names under the cover; one was my friend Mitchell. We have been friends for quite sometime, him always driving me wherever when I was without a license, always there to talk to, to drink with, and to lighten the mood. He was dating my niece at one point, but some things don't last forever. I always thought that they would get married and have little annoying children, but fate has a way of changing things. We were teammates in hockey Mitch and I, always having each other's back like brothers. Well, we pretty much are brothers in a sense; we were only line mates for one whole season, but it was a great season. Speaking of hockey, I saw my old hockey coach Mr. Weber the other day while I was working; he was all surprised that I was at work and not off to college or some trade program. He told me that I should get out and find a real job with good education, then he said, "You don't wanna work in a sawmill your whole life like me. It's not worth it." Those words I took to heart. Yea know, the fact that someone like him that I respect a lot told me that, I guess it just meant a lot; you don't always see your coaches say things like that. I guess my question to myself is where is serenity, where is where? Lost is gone and found is just around the corner, it's all just so much to think about. The pressure of the future, compelling as it sounds, is a fear; to change is easy but to grow up is a journey. Math 11, I am having troubles with it, it's too much of a fun class with some of my friends in it, always laughing and joking around, just a distraction foreseen until now. Now is after I was taken out of the room to be asked if I wanted to stay in this class, my mark being too low already. What make them judge so soon, not doing well on a few tests just because he moves too fast, it's supposed to be a class, not two smart kids that you follow. Where do we reason, when do we fake a smile just to compel that what we have is good enough, what words motivate the failure to success—they're just questions too many and too few. They will and won't change things but they will 'cause seen, big and little. And in that due point you fight for saying never, you stand up and consume your heart with one thought of what you want, you strive for perfection in life as do you on your opinions, it's all just that vigor that we love. I hardly ever stand up; I hardly ever push everything aside just to make one thing better. I sit and I wait, mouth closed, mind overrated with my emotions to just jump up and speak, but I don't and I won't. I'm afraid to be judged myself; I'm afraid to be myself, to voice my opinion is well off and under. Sitting there in class, mind escaping these walls yet again, I wish I was somewhere else; I wish I was in her arms. Who you may ask, this a girl I have never met yet really know, one that pulled my heart and reeled it in; many emotions of mine go far with her, I miss her always. Finding myself staring at her blue eyes in the morning, telling her I love her, all just a lie, when I wake up she is gone, she was never here. She, Micaela Currigan, resides five hours away in a little town, in the state of Washington. If I could be there right now, I would. I'd be on a walk with someone that sees me for me, she values what I say and her brilliance is amazing. She's one of a kind and she is my one. If I'm certain of one thing in my life, I'm certain of this. High hopes and high dreams, a love surge that flows deeply in my veins, I've never felt this way about anyone. She captures me at my best and shows me views I would never see. I'll find the road, I'll be with her for eternity as they say to those you love. Spring break, I think I'll go meet her, I hope; if not, I must keep waiting and if she never comes out, I shall die lonely, waiting for her. I wrote a poem all for her, about waiting, here I'll show you.

Atop a hill I stand
my life in the palm of my hand
moments pass and moments come
this life of mine all undone
confused and lost how I feel
framed in time with all the thoughts in mind
I'm frozen now like I was then
I miss a girl and I missed her then
I'm young; a teen
I'm supposed to be free
thoughts of her, I'm waiting
and all this time deliberating
stay or go I never know
I'm broken until the end
when she comes I'll know
It will then be time to go.

Words I wrote to a girl, a promise to always wait, and I will, she is dear and beautiful, a sweetheart of the sweetest kinds. Where do our hearts guide us? To those we love or farther away until nonexistent? When do we know we're with the right person? They should be our best friend, they should be the one that shares our joy, they should be the one that we live with forever. Divorce is an easy way out; if you marry, you should not try to change your partner. You should just embrace for all they are, they are your other half, they reason you out until there's nothing there to reason. Value this, don't give up on a slump that slowed down your heart's desire in what you once saw. Deep down you will always love them, ignorance is a flaw in love, it just hides our deeper truths. "Okay, come on do your work, stop talking and just do it," this is Mr. Bradshaw's attempt to get the class to work, his face red only for a second, as if to scare us the students into working. But who wants to work when we could talk or listen to our music? The reason I love going to school is all my friends are in one place and it's awesome; there's no feeling of conception or insecurity, our school in fact is a great place to attend, you just have to see the good things, not the bad. Every thirty seconds I find myself glancing at the clock. Time moves so slow in class, but really it's all gone right before your eyes. Some days I just want it all back, some days I just want to scream in the terror of it all, the moments we thought were just there when they're already gone as if they never existed, it's all so sad, giving up an era for another. Times compels us to accept who we are now, not who we were then. Only a few minutes now, then I got my spare, a solid block to allow us some adventure with our days in school. I always have these random thoughts of doing something different, not for everyone else just for myself, like for instance, just running into a puddle, jumping into the banks just to feel young, less mature. God I miss it, that fact that we could act stupid and have so much fun doing it without all the pressure that comes with growing up. So much joy in such a little world, referring to elementary school, running through the forest as if through a huge jungle, our imaginations were great then, no limits just dreams and the steady words behind it saying we can do it if only we try. When I think back, I don't remember what I wanted to be, I wish I could remember his thoughts but I don't, he matured into me, sad, I know, but I am just him in another way lost and confused the teenage way. *Beeeep!* Time for spare. Out of my desk, walking out I glance and see the past, the classroom, I see voice in these walls, memories, terms unclosed, crushes gone, I'm wrecked, I'm broken, stared upon as if to mock these walls with my name, I am judged day by day, it doesn't bother me, I'm in school, this is better than not trying at all, this is better than my siblings try. Out the door, all the time in the world now, I throw my bag in my locker and grab Chris, we take my car and head down to Askew's. Looks, feelings just be strong there's no pressure. If you let it escape your system, better days go unnoticed but these ones stick around I'm always asked why I wear a frown, yet I don't know. Car out of the parking lot were gone, driving slow, turning right, and finding a spot, doors locked, a paced walk, now to the door.

5

A pause then a step, the electric door slowing Chris and I down as it does to everyone, the door made almost for the elderly. The slow, near motionless seniors that shop there every day the door almost always slamming in their face, maybe they should do sprints to keep up with the future technologies that tend to slow the rest of us. I remember reading a novel, and in this novel there was all talk of only certain children living and when you reach the age of fifty you are to go to a room like an animal and be put down. Who could do such a thing, as if having no feeling just plans for a faster success in the world, a readiness to grow without the old, I thought about this when I was twelve years old or so and really we would lose the wise, we would lose the great teachings of our past, if we followed any morals toward that novel this world would have cut out our past history. Getting past both electric doors now inside Askew's, we turn right instantly I looking for my Red Bull, my daily high, and Chris, well, he's just looking for something new to drink, always looking for something funny or something related to what he likes to do. I walk over to the cooler and walking past is a shorter lady by the name of Dorothy, she's another of my managers, I always intend to give her a bad time at work, always bugging her calling her a witch, she isn't though, well, not to me. She's just someone to check in on, someone that can be honest about how you work. Often known for her attitude, yet I don't think I would enjoy working here if she didn't make it so interesting with the jokes and the humor of evil haha, she's good to have around though. "Hey, Tanner, did ya see, Red Bull went down in price," Dorothy now telling me this maybe a hint for me to piss my money away on something so insignificant but I'd rather it be Red Bull than something like heroine, something I couldn't control, something that would kill me and my loved ones along with it, drugs are just dreams wiped away. I walk over and pull out two four-packs of Red Bull, this is said to be enough to kill you four times over, I don't care though if I die it's fate, it's a choice we were willing to take, Chris sees what he likes and grabs a can with a surfer on it; he's obsessed with the theory of surfing and he hasn't even tried yet, it's a dream not a drug, and if he goes and tries it, that's all that matters, to fail after trying shows much more character, yet to try again shows courage in those eyes around you. We take our drinks to the till I pay with a twenty and a ten, the cashier giving me a dire look as if I am crazy, to try new things is not crazy though, it's genius. If everyone thought people were crazy for trying something new, we would have nothing but ignorance. Now guiding myself out, saying goodbye to the coworkers as if I just finished work for the day, back through the electric doors that we came and now running to my car as if just for fun, some excitement for our youth to devour. Hopping in my car, turning the key over, *reeee, reeee*, this a somewhat typical thing for my car to do. I pop the hood, turn the key over again and it starts, this now making me have to get out and close the hood, what a pain. Driving out of the parking lot down the road and through the one-way exit of the school, going and parking my car now, we get out and make a glance at the school then proceed on in. Nothing doing in the computer lab so we keep our restless feet moving and we head down to the library; this is where Chris's mom works, she's fair though, no favorites just equals. We walk inside past the book security scanner and Chris goes and asks his mom for some money, she of course as most mothers do grabs him some change from her purse, we then extend our walk on down to the drink dispenser. Chris puts his change in, hoping to get water but I changed that by pushing down on the apple juice button before he could choose his water, water would be a waste of money to get though, we have fountains and it's free so really I just saved him from making a poor choice. Turning around we head back toward the library and go into the gym in an attempt to work out the muscles that neither of us really have, I guess it's really just something to do, ya know. And so we sit and work out for the remainder of our spare, why I was still here I don't know, I could have called for a ride home but instead I'll take the slow, safe ride home on the bus. Still sitting there working on my lower body workout routine which is just me sitting there pushing three hundred pounds up and down with my legs, so simple yet so hard. Having a thought now that I'll go for my old record of eight Red Bull in fifteen minutes, I give it a try, downing the first pack in 6 minutes all going down pretty easy, no head rush yet, I must be good to go, drinking three more and stalling on the last, chugging it all in twelve minutes. Here it comes, the great feeling of all that blood being pushed up to my head, nose very clear as if about to bleed but it doesn't, it stays in an uncomfortable phase as if to annoy me. I love these drinks, always waking me, giving me that extra push in sports school and work, it's a weakness though knowing that it's the drink, not you pushing yourself, it's just slowly making you out of shape, a hazard that you can't even see, maybe never will until one day when you're playing basketball with your friends, your heart beats faster and faster, you collapse, falling into a dark blaze. This happened to a young boy in Ireland, so I was told by a teacher, maybe it was false information or so that's what I like to believe. Yet I think it's all true; after having more than enough Red Bull, I can feel it, my heart pumping to keep up with my oversized fast reflexes. It's not the fact that this drink can kill me; it's the fact that before it can do that, it changes me to a worse person filled with energy yet very depressed with my outcome it's almost as if it kills my ambitions, making me helpless to its can of high-priced energy that fills the void. Keeping me awake through the night and tired the next day, forcing me to buy more and more, digging my own grave day by day. Feeling all energetic now, Chris and I head back to the library him already with his apple juice and other drink in his system and I with my eight Red Bulls still deluding my body's efforts to digest it. We walk out the gym and past the guitar class that we probably should have been in since we wanted to start a band one day. They're starting to sound pretty good after such a short time, this a little regret of mine, having a guitar at home that one I rarely use. Consumed with dust, it sits alongside my lyrics, those that I had one day dreamed of singing in front of millions of people, bringing everyone together in one place just to listen to my words; it's a dream, not something that's around the corner. Chris and I now reach the library doors; we step inside and pulsate around. His mom Nancy tells us that the school won't be getting the money to get a video camera for the school; this is what Mr. Bradshaw has been talking about for quite some time. I find that kinda sad, looking forward to teaching film now just crushed away in tainted ash. Not only that but I was also looking forward to it, wanting to make a short film that was serious, unlike my familiar dry-humor copycat films that I make with my friends. I have this interest in films, either acting in them or writing or just having fun with a camera; it would never be about the fame. it would be the integrity of art in film that was made seen because of what we envisioned what we saw that made a certain look stand up. Chris says he's going to try and get in the computer lab, so I just go for a loser lap around the school. Slow steps taking my time, there's no rush. Walking along in the grade 8 hallway, I spot a girl sitting on one of the benches—red hair, green eyes.

This is Colbie Franson; she's in a pretty loyal hockey family, priding themselves on that, a great deal of hockey skill passed on to her two brothers Cody and Cain. Colbie is a figure skater, a great one at that; she has this great personality that will catch your eye no matter who you are. Don't talk rude to her or 'cause infliction, it could be like playing with fire. One of the best smiles and one of the purest hearts, Colbie's going to make someone really happy one day; I value her very much as a friend. We used to just say hello and stuff like that, but then we talked and brought up feelings, point of views on life and past relationships, trying to mend each other's low spirits. I only wish I knew her longer than I have; I only wish I saw the amazing person that she is before now. She's simple and sweet and very, very unique, she's Colbie. I sit and ask her what she's up to. "Oh nothing, Tanner, just working on some of my biology." I stay a while longer, grasping the moment that we actually sit and talk together since it's really very few. "Please listen for your end-of-school announcements, *beep!*" I say later to Colbie with school now over. I walk down to the gym and grab my backpack. Brian is there. "Hey, Tanner, you wanna stay after and shoot around for a bit?" I explain to him that I can't today, that I have to take the bus, and that I'm already in a hurry to get in the line. Off I go, an average rate of speed, walking down the halls, stopping off at my locker, grabbing my homework that I probably won't do, off again, out the front middle entrance straight on out and now standing in line ready to head back to Malakwa. Always regarded as greasy even just a joke for riding the school bus and living in Malakwa, I enjoy where I live though no one's opinions are going to change that; they don't live there so they to see the beauty in peace in quiet. The first bus now comes; this bus takes the kids from Six Mile home. The bus, not even half full, almost seems like a waste of money for the school district; they, I'm sure, could easily just let the few students' carpool saving money for a better budget. Here now comes the turtle bus, this being a good name since Kathy isn't the fastest of bus drivers. The line being pushed back, following the rules of the bus driver Kathy and the supervising teacher Mr. Beeftink, now as we get the signal from Kathy and start climbing aboard, we hear the words of Mr. Beeftink repeatedly, "KEEP OFF THE GRASS!" We're all used to it now; it's just that simple reminder of boarders in our school ensemble, finding a seat near the back, staring out a partly fogged window, half sun half fog to stare at, with bitter clouds following over. The bus door closing and us heading off, the ride home always something different to see, some angle of something that you don't see till now, that second of knowing that you drive past something every day yet today you noticed it, it wasn't just that boring sign or building, it was like seeing it for the first time and you felt like you were in a whole new place. It's in those moments where you feel confused yet so alive, not knowing if what you just saw is something new or not. It's a mystery; it grabs ahold of our thoughts, and it twists them till we believe and we use our imagination. It feels like there's less potholes on the way home, whether this is true or not I don't know. Either way, I wish there wasn't any; it would make for a nice soothing ride. Reaching the start of the four lanes now, tons of traffic pass the school bus, leaving a big trail of dust to get through. Helplessly sitting, cramped with my knees digging into the seat, slowly coming to its first stop, the bus finds its standstill motion, lights flashing, stop sign popping out, the signal to get off and seats emptied the vacant steps of people getting off soon arousing the rest. Pulling up now to cross the highway, the bus merges on and crosses, Kathy takes a right then straight on out to my stop. Lights flashing, stop sign popping out yet again, I sit ready to jump up, just waiting for the signal to get off the bus and get home inside to a place that rarely changes a place that doesn't screw with my thoughts like the ride home. I see the signal as I gradually walk forward now from the back to the front, stepping over shoes that belong to someone's feet, reaching the door now, Kathy with her gesture of goodbye and I with mine, getting signaled to cross the street and stepping through the café door now. "Hey, Tanner, how was your day?" My mom's usual words when I get home from well anything, I reply back with good and continue into the house, stepping into the computer room, turning it on, and throwing my backpack to the ground. Just settling in now, my mom shouting, "Can you go and put the wood in the wood shed," all the little things that put off what we really want to do just for a moment but it's still time gone, not wasted, just gone. I go out and move the wood; it only takes a few seconds then it's done, chores and tasks holding us back, yet do they not give us something? A chance to grow, a chance to have responsibility, they're something that helps uplift our age and our position as a teenager. Back inside now in front of my computer screen wasting away, talking to my friends online, listening to music and typing out song lyrics, that's all I ever seem to do when I get home, and what for, it's not like my songs are good; it's all just wasted time. I turn the music up fairly loud, I go to my room and just sit there, glancing at the wall I think about it all, this life that I have the posters of people I dream to be, covering this image of my wall. That's not me though, that's not Tanner Croft, never will be; I take comfort in that. I don't think I could ever handle fame, falling in with the wrong crowd, overdose after overdose finding myself in rehab only just after getting out, that's a life I can't live, ever. It makes me wonder about my brother's hopes; did he ever think about it all and how he could fail his dreams? That's something I can't answer, only one person can one person who knew what was going on inside and that's himself, it's sad, falter your dream to throw it away for nothing. Flip a coin, that's your fate. That seems what it's like, but it's not. Just apply yourself, that's something I want to do. I want to prove people wrong—I want to write a book and publish it; I want to make an album and sell it. I have dreams, but there's something else, something that I want that I'm not sure I can do and that's teaching. I have all these abilities to play sports, but I don't want that as a PE teacher. I want that feeling of sharing what you know with your pupil; it's exciting, it's great, and it's holding me back. I'm scared 'cause I know so little and I can't take failure or new beginnings. Well, that's just who I am—shy, quiet, often unseen. Something I can't be as a teacher, I need to be the center of attention. Damyen my brother wanted to be a teacher, but his teacher said he wouldn't be good at it and now look where he is. I think he would have been a great teacher; if he just blocked those negative thoughts out maybe he would be one today. Opinions will change people, judgment will change people, this thought drives society to a wielding fire of inequality, one that weakens our system of life. If we blocked it out, if we didn't listen, we would thrive and they would fall.

6

Often I find myself singing, always in the most obscure moments; it's nice though, a feeling that you don't care if it's bad 'cause it's you—you're just being yourself, living, feeling free. I'm not a rock star, there's no media here, there's no one here to tell me if I'm off-key or the sound isn't good enough for them. I relish what I write; to sing is even better, a feeling of accomplishment and a feeling that maybe one day I'll make that album. Sales don't matter; it's just something to be put away, a keepsake, something with meaning telling everyone in this world that I can do more than you think. I have dreams, won't reach many, but I will with some and when I do I'll look down to my children and I'll tell them that I had dreams some happened and some didn't but I tried, that's what matters, that's what counts in this lifetime. Music still playing away and I'm still there thinking on it all; it's always been this way since I was little, turning the music way up and just releasing all that pressure of what hurts and what angers me. I'm sure, however, at the age of three I was just screaming with the music, nothing made sense then, still doesn't, but I'm starting to see it now, I'm starting to accept things, I'm still scared about it all, but that's okay. I think that's how it's supposed to be until you're ready to accept who you are as a person, I'm just not ready yet, I'm not ready to accept life's challenges, and one day I'll have to face that fear and grow out of the shadow that overtakes my spirits. Why do we as teenagers drink to keep or make an image for ourselves? What greater notion does it give us? I remember always wanting to get my friend drunk, finally he did and I wasn't even there to see it, yet I didn't feel happy for him; it's just a weakness, a fake notion of a good time that leads to harmful deaths. If I lost myself for drinking, if I hurt someone drinking, if I chose to do drugs drinking, then I am dead. I am a skeleton fracture of a broken teenager that is trying to fit in and might not do that in my efforts. Often I see myself watching those MADD commercials and really they make sense; I mean, have you ever seen a mother bury her son, did you ever look into her eyes after the funeral or years later 'cause there's something missing, her son was taken by a driver or maybe he was the driver but either way those tears show compassion, something we all take for granted, something that shows that greater emotion. A knock coming off my bedroom door. "What do you want for supper 'cause I have to leave for a meeting in a few minutes?" "I'll just wait till you get back, Mom, it's no big deal." Really, though, it is this big deal; every day I come home so hungry and I wait and I wait and then at 10:00 p.m. I'll sit down and eat something I'm sure it's not good for me but I do it, I'm busy, I'm a teen, we're either all fat, average, or anorexic and we're all picked apart because of it. I know students that can't even look at themselves in the mirror without thinking they're fat; the sad thing is that they're not fat, they just pick up a magazine and think that they need to look a certain way. All of these things make people feel so terrible and depressed about themselves, what's the point in it all? So many of us are not made to look like celebrities, why can't we all just realize that and move on; I mean, what are you gonna do, get a plastic surgeon to look at you and make you something you're not? To do that is just making you a monster; you're some lab rat, some person that is not real anymore, and you have to look at yourself every day in the mirror and ask if it was worth it. There's better ways, more natural ways. It just takes longer than a day of surgery—do yoga, do fitness, test your body, and try to live a better lifestyle. Don't just go throw up in a bucket because you don't think you look good enough for one person 'cause deep down you do just need to realize your potential as a person. Don't let a magazine choose your life, let yourself choose for you. I hear the door slam shut, I walk to the window and see my mom drive away to her meeting, now what to do? Home alone is like a forbidden freedom that escalates on a curvy path; we know they're gone, but when will they come home? We never know therefore we must be hasteful with our fun. I go sit down and look for a basketball or hockey game on the TV. Clicking through I find nothing, so I pace around my house looking for something, anything to do. I go back to the computer, sit in front of it for a while, just waiting for something to happen. Maybe that's what's wrong with me; I just wait for it all to happen, that change, that specific alternation in my life where I realize I can't look back 'cause it's gone. I am always just waiting, never at the right time nor moment, nothing clicks unless it's out of the blue and something I can't control, something like fate. I now look at the time and see it's near 5:00 p.m. I go back to my room and sit for a while, staring at that wall, a picture of a microphone, under is the word *dream*. I put this up recently; it gives me something to think about every morning I wake up—the thought that we can all choose what we want to do with our present state to shape our future. We can't wait; we need to grasp every second of every day of every moment in our lives to give us a better chance in this world, a chance to grow to be somebody and to make others around us believe. I have all these things I could be and do, yet I wait and I think that it won't matter ten years from now but it will, God, it will and will give us something more to thrive and live for; the last thing we need is some lame-ass reason to kill ourselves. To falter over a girl or a friend, to think that we're not wanted in the world when the truth is we're just not trying to be the person we first set out to be. Many of us don't yet know who we're going to be, but that is no excuse to wait and gawk in a corner as if to find refuge at some bitter time in our life when we need to step up and grasp the cornerstone, the hinge that binds our will to make ourselves something. Up on my feet again, I throw on a pair of joggers and throw on my hoody, put on my tattered old runners, and head out the door. A cool wind blows over me, clouds gathering above the silence, then a drop of rain falls, more and more it comes, the soothing falling rain. I start my run, the great feeling of running in the run. Those uplifting moments when you feel as though you have everything in front of you and you grab it all with every step you take, I often feel this way—that push or drive that builds up somewhere in the back of our mind. This is my run, my thoughts always coming and going, emotions drained, just running away trying to find new ways of outlook on life and how I come to terms with the things in it. Atmospheres are always changing, challenges will grow; that security that I felt in high school, it will all go away. I'll be the center of attention in an empty room, I'll crash and burn, a failure in the making that's trying to find his way. What dreams to get me to this moment did I myself leave behind, little time for goofing off, a summer to waste then college, what fate shall I embrace, will I even go to college? I don't know, I'm so scared I wish I had more time to see it all again, it was all so fast, I lost control couldn't keep up and now the memories I made they're all a haze. I look at my yearbooks and see a boy who lost his smile and matured on his way. Our parents think it's easy, always badgering on what I should do with my life when really the terrifying reality is I don't know what I wanna do. I can't see it yet, I just wanna leave, get away for a year or two, I want to find that boy that I left behind a long time ago, the one that saw things so perfectly and embraced everything he had in his life 'cause that was the best he could do and he did it well, I miss that side of me. Soaked in rain, a quiet smile over my face as if to laugh and enjoy the moment in the rain, fresh, pure rain, leaping over puddles and cracks in the road, it's not race, no rare occasion, just a boy in the rain. Along the road and up past the church, around the corner and across the railway, crossing slowly, now I trot along, finding my way on the path of the road, taking me home and yet beyond the world's reaches of beauty. There's so much unseen here, so much more—a childhood walking this road around and home again, a filling journey that inspires the soul, one that realistically defies the greater places that are seen by all the world instead of hidden in captivity like this in such a place. Running slower now, step after step coming to the wooden car bridge, I now freeze and stand still, the cool breeze of the Eagle River walking over me and onto the valley. The refreshment just burying itself onto me, breathing it in deeper and deeper, clearing my head and bringing subtle thoughts onto thee. It's such a perfect place to live, the beauty pulling you to the malice of a river streaming under a bridge. There's that sandbar that your friend and yourself fished at all summer, covered with the cool shade of the tall cedars. After here, you wander back across the train tracks; beyond here you see an empty field—it's an old baseball field. My mom played here long ago, yet it feels like yesterday that I sat and watched them play their slow-pitch games, tall grass and weeds now linger here like a lost past with no intention of coming back, the good times gone yet maybe just clouded over by skeptical reasons of an aged-over community. Childhood here is of the traditional kind, not in the sense of technology, just in the terms of our endeavoring young adventures. We all know each other here, all go to school together, we're close, we put the word *community* to good use, and that's a great thing. I pick up a rock and throw it to the water from the bridge, a light splash sounds as well as rings of a scratched surface of water—the ripple effect on a reflective surface. A great writer once wrote something that we find a notion that it's good based on a name, not words, we block out the few facts in this statement. Shakespeare, Frost—great writers, yet I think there were and are better ones out there they're just not seen, they're hidden by what a higher figure thinks is correct and thinks is better, but truth be told that creativity cannot be held back in chains with the past. Shakespeare and Frost are just a footnote in what people in this world can do, and isn't that the point to it all? To better ourselves with previous pastimes and not be pushed down by a voice of opinion that prefers the past? This is to my ideal I am portraying to my English teachers, is always not seen as good enough; my writing always lacked what theirs had. It's unfair, it's obscene to think comparison is eligible. My point is why can't we all just be heard? Why can't we let everyone who wants to write and not be put down for it? Why can't we all believe that? My face now red and I breathing harder than when first starting, turning around, wind now at my back, I glance at the empty road and start from where I came. Graduation is coming up soon; I didn't grad last year as I already stated. I was an escort though to a Ms. Ashley Cox; she's one of the funniest girls I know, always laughing at nothing really, but that's my sense of humor too, oh so dry haha. It was pretty sweet taking that bighearted comedienne to grad, one of those memories you don't wanna forget 'cause it's with the best of the people you know and adore. After grad that night at 2:00 a.m., a few of us went to my friend Dirk's—that's where I was staying the night; we all just sat by a fire talking, having a few beers, good times. Most of us stayed there till 10:00 a.m. and then Dirk and I walked down to the basketball court and shot a few hoops then passing out for a bit by the swings, we awoke and Dirk called his mom for a ride. She came and he was a little hesitant about getting in the car well until he threw up, then he got in, it was so funny. I'm not sure what it's gonna be like this year at grad, who I'm going to get as an escort or if I'll even win a scholarship. I know I'm not a nerd, a smarter person, but I don't think I'd want that. I just like being normal. Screwing up is okay; it's something we go through as human beings. However, I'm still not so clear on graduating. One class holds me back right now; it has for the past three years—Math 10 Principles. That's a hard one, but this year is looking good. I'm trying to accept it all; the fun's over, the goofing off, it has to stop. It's hard sometimes when the laughing gets out of control, but I need to focus right; it's my future at stake, not my past. Ultimate season is also starting up here soon; we started our first team last year, and it was some of the best fun I've ever had on a sports team. I can play it again this year, yet I dunno if I want to. All my friends and teammates tell me to play and really I've wanted to for the past year, but something's missing—the will to play the game is gone. I don't think I want to; I'd rather graduate than play a game for one more year. I'd just be too busy with it all, and golf team is up again too so I would be really busy. If I do however, then I shall make the best of it one last hurrah at a fun sport. Drenched in cool, pure water fallen from the sky, I slow up and walk for a little ways. Already passing the corner and the church, I walk into the school boundaries and go sit under the sheltered concrete pad by the basketball court. No shivers, no deep breaths, just calm thinking for a young boy, the moment of aspiration is now, thoughts of doubt are left behind. I climbed a hill and a mountain; I now stand atop bearing a flag with my name, Tanner Brodie Fenton Croft. This is my step, there's no looking back here, what's been done has been done. I am what I am and that's who I will continue to be; confidence will inspire me, and I will grow to certain proportions at heart. The only option now is moving forward. Just recently over spring break, I went on a little road trip to the country music town of Merritt. It wasn't all that I expected; I thought there would be more. I found that there was little fun there, and my friends disappeared as people that I thought I knew of. My best friend became a completely different person I felt as if I was pushed into a hole here and made not to talk or to be seen. It was oh so depressing, yet when we arrived back home, I found myself revitalized and better, a common use of energy flowing now. I don't know what overwhelmed me on that trip, but something did and it hurt. To be trapped in a place where I should be happy, there's something wrong with that, deeply wrong. That moment is gone though, an obstacle that was overcome not with joy, but just to finish.

C.L.O.N.E.

Sun gone; shadow covers this land
Humans vanished, what happen to life span
Time lines erased our future a blur
Wire, cords, electricity formed
The age of domination; technology born
The cancers inside us destroyed who we were
They took it back, they took over
Their brains in our bodies
So identical, yet so impure
A wasted world so conformed
No more emotions, feeling it left out the door
We wanted a world of peace
Now having it, we can't see it
Who we were is gone

This is a self-image of what's wrong with us, the humans, no fun we are. Sure, there's a few people that party, but we're all children of some parent in the world, so why do we change? Look at the title of the poem "Child Lost On New Equality," where did it go, the fun? It's all a lie, isn't it. I mean, I was watching an old 1950s movie, and it was too surreal, too happy. This world isn't happy land; there's a hell of a lot more feeling than happiness in the world, some that we may never experience, but it's there. And what's the deal with maturity? I mean, most our parents are some clone work—work, nap, work, sleep. I don't want my life to be that way, so much work, so little fun. Childhood left them; I don't wanna lose it myself. Grad's coming soon, who are you taking? Always the question on my friend's mind when we bring it up or so. Are you actually gonna grad this year, someone else will comment. No, he's gonna be here till he's old. That hurts, yet I conceal it to myself. I'm always the joke, the underachieving nongraduate. I wrote a song about it as well.

Nongraduate

Passing through these doors again
A new year begins; I'm without the others
My friends, it's my 13th year and I'm
just that same kid, that same boy

I'm an underachieving nongraduate
Say goodbye to the money kid
Say goodbye to home kid
It's time to grow; time to change
Feeling older every day
My color is gone, faded away
I'm not that boy I used to be
I'm growing up too fast to see
It haunts me slowly and then
Time just trickles on and on

I'll still be that same
underachieving nongraduate
In their eyes, in my eyes
Just a kid that failed

I'm an underachieving nongraduate
Say goodbye to the money kid
Say goodbye to home kid
It's time to grow; time to change

What will change, what will happen when all youth leave home? Will our elders give thanks, will they throw us out like bums, will we fall apart on our own trying to find our way, crumbling under pressure, finding influence in low-paying jobs and a bottle of cheap whiskey? It's a fear to end up like this, to fall to the bitter smile of the sun before the day has yet to relinquish itself. What turmoil, what tremors the shaking of a small boy lost in his journey, afraid of where he's going. This is me; I'm comprehending paths and ways, yet fall short of my own expectations. What's next is yet to be determined by the heart of the boy.

7

I pick myself and my thoughts up off the pavement and walk around out to the front of the school, step after step slowly reaching somewhere, the exit out of the boundaries I think. Ah, so many cracks in this brittle pathway with its chalk drawings and painted on Four Square forms.

This the path of children, one end leading to the exit, the other to their imagination, the forest, field, and court. So many adventures, so many journeys, so many memories. You will always remember those childhood days, your first crush on the swing set next to you and you in awe, she thought you were just making a funny face at her so she ran off and still finds you to be odd, yes, the good old days, haha. Walking under the sheltered gap of the two school buildings, past down the open concrete slope, the wording of the bus line fading away from the winter's snow through the fence line now reaching to my pocket for my iPod, I grasp it and put it on, blasting my tunes I begin my run again.

Dusk now joins my backside as we wander along this road back home, passing over three houses and onward I break alongside the highway's feet, some fierce glow standing inside now staggering out, giving more kick to every step of every stride I take there's no thinking no pain it's all just this push that makes me feel deserving of being here. Collaboration of the mind with my wits in my body and my mind empty to the course, slowing I am now, here at the intersection, the lights shining, my friend is gone for now. I pause the music, alert of this surrounding, I am grasping some strange realization so I look in the back of my mind, it's my picture frame I stand in awe of this view—a highway intersection in Malakwa, rows of lights filling the void of darkness and I with haste find a view that endears my heart. *MHHHHHH, MHHHHHH!* A semi driving by, honking his horn loudly resets my focus, I unpause my song and continue on in diligent fashion, slower than before with less stride in every step along the gravel sideline of the road. Nearly at my house now, I start walking, not a slow walk though it's a good pace, faster than my mom walks and that's a fair pace, I cross the street just in front of the café and walk around back. I open the white door that's been through a hell of a battle with my dogs, scratch marks all over, I step inside and go sit down in front of the computer. "Tanner? Tanner was that you? Are you home?" "Yea, Mom, I'm right here. Why, what's up?" "Mitchell called, he wants you to call him back." "Okay, Mom, will do, thanks." I reach to the right, grab the phone, and call him. "Hey, is Mitch there?" "Sure, thanks . . . Hey, man, what ya call for? A party, I dunno, man, who we going with? Your cousin Andrew and Al, sure, I'll just bring thirty bone and crash at your place, 'kay great, I'll talk to you in a few minutes. I just gotta change, peace." I spin out of the chair and rush to my room; I throw on my Red Sox jersey and another pair of my low-cut jeans. I flip on a hat, tell my mom the plan, get the usual lecture don't drink it's not good for ya, me question it all just say yes to make her somewhat secure with the idea of her youngest son going out. I've always been the youngest with my brothers and sister being so far apart in age than me; my mom, because of this, would never let me go out and would always freak on me for drinking. I grew accustomed to it though so did she, I'm sure, especially after raising the lot of us. Rushing out of the house and to my car, I'm now on my way, back the way I had just came. To one of those three houses that are now on my left I go. I parked my car in the driveway and walked into my best friend's house, I've known the kid forever and, well, his parents too so we're all pretty close which is comforting since, well, I'm always staying the night over there after having a few. Knowing where Mitch is, I just walk downstairs to his room. Finding all the guys playing the Xbox, I grab a seat and watch as they play Call of Duty 4. "Hey, man, what's up?" "Nothing much, man, I just got in from a run when you called." This conversation was short-listed, I found myself in front of the liquor store with a little wallet waiting in the car, hinged in between the two seats of my friend's Civic, my knee shaking as if I was in a hurry, but I wasn't; it's just some moderate movement of comfort some reliable position that tells me it's good but it wasn't good, nothing close to comfort, I was completely cramped sitting in a car waiting for my booze, the sad part is I was cramped by an empty seat I mean come on why haven't I pushed it up just a bit yet. The booze, of course, was being bought for me; if only I had a fake ID, I wouldn't be sitting here I would be in there getting exactly what I wanted up to par, not a hole in one though, not with the selection so limited and the green fairy absinthe, not even a hallucinogenic, we only have the 75 percent kind here in North

America and, well, if it's not even the real thing, what's the point. I'm sure I'd be smacked by my mother for even thinking of this, my lecture of a nonhallucinogenic drink.

~

The bar-framed door of the liquor store now opening, so simple, a few boards some metallic wire and a big lock, not quite yet rusted but soon will, an antique of a door made only in last few years, a joke on the footprints of doors. My friends coming out of that door and now stepping inside the green chrome four-door Civic, "Here ya go, buddy," passing me my beers and a five-dollar bill of change, the bill, however, was partially tattered in some areas which made me wonder if I could use it later in the week. It has now occurred to me that a man of shadowy death has taken from this town now meaning of this to me is not shown but in later times I will see it dearly, those faces which once stood so jolly and proud will go unseen and unheard of for the next twenty to thirty years in which I was supposed to come home to those people's greetings and remarks of change and age, instead terms of death, grieving an enviable pain, one to which gives much awareness to pastimes and darkened beacons to which we purposely forgot to share and open up with to our surrounding peoples. I always despise the fashioned look of a funeral, is it not a celebration of life, then why the black suits and dresses of a shallow grave, why not a shining sun to the highest corners of the world, why not bright florescent clothes, something that says celebration of life, not the modern death seen from the 1950s? Key turned, music now shouting through my ears, "What is Love" playing over and over again on our way to the so-called party. "So who even told you about the party?" "I got my resources," Alan Mack claimed, a few minutes after this his cell rang. "Hey, what's up? . . . Oh nice, umm my friends and I are just heading to your party . . . what? Ah, why? That's lame, 'kay, well, if plans change, give me a shout later." An awkward silence telling us all indirectly that, well, there won't be a party tonight. "Well, what time is it? Nine oh eight . . . Well, let's go drunken bowling," a long pause with unjust balance than a simple fret of words, yea sure, might as well the guys all persisting on this thought of fun. Off we go, slamming our beers, *clink, clink*, cheers! Over the car bridge in Sicamous, leading us to Salmon Arm, should we leave here with a tragedy bearing our helpless souls, shall we falter on the bends and curves of the darkened highway road. I don't know what would be so bad about a death like this, the enviable pain from the ones we would leave or just, well, the fact that the bearer of my sir name would not come to be named, however I'd die with some of the best guys I know, what a way to go. We won't die though, too much to live for especially when we yet don't know what that is, a question unanswered to many. I've come to a conclusion that well among many things, I'm well a fuckup, yes, I have passions and dreams, skills and knowledge, I could be bigger and stronger yet I am unjust with these and a path of FUCK UP is fine, I've learned to see that those words belong to them. The them is the judgmental many, I'd love to say few, but I can't contain them like that, I am one of them I know because I judge so many, so many times a day, she's fat, I wonder why she wears black oh I know she's fat, what makes me better? Nothing, I just choose not to care, to care is to fail and, well, if I cared about them calling me or labeling me as a fuckup then I wouldn't be that boy I thought I was, the one that didn't care about what the so-called better said, I am fine and well as far as I see it what they think can't be appealed to me, what I have and see is before the holder which is me.

~

Sheer brilliance watching a bottle smash, the flares of light bursting from the rustic-once yeast-filled smothered-in-water capsule, if only our heart could break as these, we would find no more meaning in love or touch, just feeling lost in a bottle of emotions. Fathomed at looks if only our appearances didn't matter all the time we would all be good enough all the weight-loss magazines thrown out, the fashion model seen destroyed and the clone model would stand in despair as mobs of equals crushed empires of look and plastic beauty, if you're fat you're fat, if you're skinny you're skinny, if you're normal then, well, there is no normal, we're all just weird, crazy at times but if looks didn't cease to exist and beauty is a word used rarely to make one's heart expire to the needed rush of consumption, then we are fine. I would find redemption in a place of look less matter without the perfume and fur coat just a smile and a hollow eye that says it all. I lay back and think of a thought I love, some reasoning to scream, just to grab the microphone walk around an empty house screaming, no attention, no shameful changes in voice it's just a picture-perfect image of a boy screaming, not for his mom but for himself, screaming to dream to show the world who you really are to be somebody. It's a thought of my inner self waking this heartless teenager up before he crashes his hopes, his dreams, his intentions as they were once planned. Bright lights causing a fuss with all of us, some random driver drawing our concentration of the car ride with their high beams, still no death tone tragedy, still no buzz, six beers gone I have a feeling that when I stand it will hit me harder than this tight squeeze of seating I am perspiring to, not a lot though just enough to well drive me crazy. Cheers after cheers, car still on the road, no forced appeal off, just driving on, clear dusk road line's in view no fog no hydroplaning on this dry land set of road. Where is that girl from your dreams? Is he here in this town in the next or miles away, what depths, what measures can we take to seek such an enviable object? One that finds you in pain the next day seeing that what you saw the night before may never happen and never really did happen, it hurts on those mornings, and if she is here what holds back on speech? Is it your friendship view, the loyal friend that would never want more with you, it's hard to face that rejection that loss of just a dream's reality. One day when you return home conception could change, views of matters such as these could find higher lifts and very little lows, and what of those perfect days when you wish that girl was the one, when you wish her smile was your sun, I'd love a lifetime of those days just to talk and be near such a personality, the only comfort gained however is pain. We've all been there, we've all had our drought, they appear to lead us on and then, well, they're gone. My arm brushed up gingerly upon the window ledge, my blue eyes prying onto rocky walls of mountainsides, it's a view, it's a view, one never need be broken just sought after by all sorts of mismatched peoples in this world, searching for that land mass of inspiration, well, the Okanagan has that it has its mystery but its history is oh so dull, why couldn't we have some big icon something great to remember our past something other than boring inventions or history that no one cares about unless you're, well, inhuman to the forms of man's greater accomplishments.

~

To the stoplights where we sit waiting, just waiting, for that light to turn green, not to race just to maintain the order of the road, the dominated machine system which I'm sure has caused more than one accident a year just on faulty use. What will happen when we rely too much on the human machine that does not beat as one of us? Not terminator, just flawed machines that can 'cause death amongst mankind, I mean if we start to fail from technology then maybe we would have been better off without it, from what it's looking like we would have been a lot better without it, sad, really, how something we create could lead to our demise.

8

Laugh after laugh I'll rid humor, some common form in every boy, not the immature kind just the drunken showboat kind with the cockiness of a preppy rich kid something that we don't really have is money, something that I don't want is money in my hand. I'm the kind that sees the opportunity to spend what I have in one to two days, this doesn't make for a great savings account, as a matter of fact I'm often just labeled as broke from poor usage of spending. Straight we go down the inclined road taking a left and finding ourselves in the hollow emptiness of the bowling alley parking lot. It's almost a pastime, the bowling scene, never really noticed anymore, and seen as a fat man's sport to many, there used to be one in Sicamous just a two laner but that's gone now, the syfiling hardwood and polished lanes the loud bang of metal on wooded puppets the greater though of a Friday night in our town thrown out in dismay, leaving us with another secondhand store in a first-rate hockey town. Now in waiting for my tied to turn, let the red wash away, let the eerie discomfort rise out onward and let some deep incision guide your fate to a matter which lies deep within your wonders. It's rather cultivating the eraser headstone getting rid of many useful hangouts and devouring what always seemed as a hidden joy only really shown on those Fridays of nights, when you're lost and oh so livid you come to terms with one knowing factor of heart ship in the deeper thoughts there are only few places that can inscribe your forget less soul no antics of immortality, even when that place is gone your inscription of past will remain, "forever here" a captivating slogan I saw on a box at work, some significant meaning to me yet some random wording of endearing minds if to stimulate a tired workmen's day. Out of the car and now walking to the concrete stair entrance, old, frail some bitter paleness of this sick old man of an entrance, one of the weaker looking entrances in the world yet he's friendly something that says welcome in. We walk in leaving our beer in the car and our shoes at the door, the lights still their regular self, cosmic bowling hadn't started yet. Terms of definement nothing more nothing less, youth is right now slowly it comes and goes but it's there, immaturity that slow sense of childhood pleasure and what echoes in the distance? The familiar ringing of an ancient phone call, one from a friend that said they would keep in touch but never did. That's going to be one of the hardest things after high school, keeping in touch with all of them. The regrets of saying goodbye to them and not getting their number, thinking that you may have it in your address book but you don't, you know very well that you don't; it's a mistake a fearful one at that. To lose touch all meaning of them, your friends, my mom always told me you have to try hard to keep in touch now I know what she means, and your new friends over the years can never replace your old memories, your old school memories it's just a world you're never going to want to let go. We've paid, now wearing our clown shoes of a post modern '80s link, the cosmic lights begin as do we. White shirts glowing with a passion to smile to the moons highest views. Growing outcomes with a number system of odd and even, the chances of life and death, the betting feuds that go on in a day of violence and deception. Roll a dye and be shot, lose all your money, lose your family flip a coin and your world flips upside down and for what a few thousand dollars just because you can't apply yourself and get a real job to gamble your life away on something so much more with flawless talents obscene to most even you, the treasury you take with the gambling lie. Find who you're meant to be not a fraud not a puppet of foreign eyes cast to a stone to a lake, to sink to the bottom never getting air, to linger motionless in a life you were not to have. Find moments to cast, to stow find love find regret find your life and you will find a better person; one of accomplishment and one of failure, no one will see your past tense failures if you yourself justly ride them out. We are all people of means, the loses and regrets can be found all over but love now that is one in a million. In a waiting 'cause I have seen another, something that sparks me close to home, close to heart. Our screen now on and our lane a flare, we in perfect stride sit and stare, for a moment or two we just look at it, the five pins mounted on string, some amount of feet ahead of the flush beauty of a lane floor, it was a moment of aw when those lights came on and the music put us in a trance to bowl, with haste we fine away out of glance and play the game we came to play. Each of us throwing a ball none of us however with a strike, the first game would continue this way for some time. Ya know I hadn't thought of it much but I'm going to grad soon, I find great fear in that, the years gone by so fast and so sudden, the great discomfort in leaving a heartfelt school. The day of grad with the excitement and nerves, a few kids drunk just to cross the stage; I one plus everyone's age this being my year thirteen but my eyes will be elsewhere. Looking at a girl white with that blond hair and those deep blue eyes, her beauty will strike my pulse of a charmed heart; I am sure we will glow together. I'll take her hand for the day getting lost in those eyes alone, no fears with her, just some moral comfort and belief in myself, she is a breathless wonder so take a deep breath before losing yourself in her beautiful ways. She is Shelby Franson a heart ache that keeps me smiling; Colbie is her cousin if you were wondering due to the last name. The two are very adventurous and gullible together, hahaha; that's okay though, just makes for good entertainment and a solid laugh.

~

Friends and foes, weaker links to our reasoned talents, a world of falling until we choose, choose to stand rather than sit to push back on something we couldn't control before, something that overwhelms to the fewer days in our lives. I got my report card the other day; it was pretty simple. It said I was a failure, all I need this year is Math 10 Principles and no one seems to get that that's all I want. If I could just get math and actually graduate with that comforting feeling knowing that I'm just a failure in their eyes and not mine, I'm fine with that, I could go into film, I could teach PE, I could coach a fair bit of sports and I could cook, but I don't know what I want and I sure as hell know I don't need some damn Geography 12 to fulfill my hopes. My cooking marks are an A, my physical education is at an A, and I make short films and act in this little short films I transcribe to make with my friends just so that over a weekend we could have a few sit-down and say, "Damn, now that's funny, hahaha." But the film thing is great in other ways like this one time I played it at the talent show in front of the school and it made them happy, so I did my job and it felt good, also I entered some of my short films in our little film festival. I'm not sure how it's gonna go—that's next week—the two are funny, but I made this third one with my friend Andrew, like a serious one with some means and weight over laughter just 'cause, well, I wanted a change. We can't all change from comedy to serious; none of my other friends wanted anything to do with it, I was kinda disappointed 'cause I want something good, I wanna write a script or a book one day, something that takes what one person feels and thinks and shows the world how some things are seen and how some things are in their eyes. I started writing a book just recently; I'll glance at this writing and think how I come up with it 'cause it's weird, let me tell ya; after all, I'm supposed to be the stupid kid from Malakwa, right, the one that plays sports and is seen as an asshole; but that's okay. We're all entitled to our opinion; I'd just like my writing to be seen.

In the middle of a parking lot there sits a tree, small in stature but will grow with time, a perfect picture if only the cars and concrete weren't locked around in place of what used to be. If I held an eraser, I'd remove the tree from what looks as utmost extinction; I suppose though it gives the elders some gesture of natural comfort. Though the mountainside sits in perfect view, captivating to you and I, the country gleaming with certain distinction will grasp our eyes on what to be a day of terror in the hearts of most summer dwellers. The snow, you see, had been now falling in this of modern April—such beauty, such shade, no color, it is all a fade with haste purity and passion of those unknown. I right there down smug sitting on a bench of oak, it's faded worn of its oils and sits in with dark intentions under me. Snow melting as falling too I'm drenched a soul pondered to few, my alliance leans toward the sun. A flock of crows to my left, the sidewalk is filled with them, no garbage lingerers on these paths their darkened eyes stare and watch, smiling in eerie silence with no understanding of who I am and what people see me as. I, William Petinger, am an uncontrolled disease, a cancer-filled twenty-one-year-old, once dreams held in hand was forced to drop and shatter them one by one, the cancer took them away. Now I sit day by day wondering what could have been, so young yet so finished in this life of mine, the doctors say I could get better If I fight back, it's just all so painful, and those eyes watching sitting and staring judging my intentions to live or die. I never asked for cancer; it just came up one day. It was just supposed to be a checkup, not a life-altering change, some intentions forced onto me, something I don't need. I'll never forget that day the phone call to come in to the doctor's office, that drive hoping I don't have it wanting to never have to face that pain. Sitting in the lounge waiting to go in, I told my mother to wait there; it was something I had to find out alone. Walking those steps, I counted eighteen; this was a moment one that shaped a change in events. I pushed the loosened door open and took a seat; I sat waiting, twiddling my thumbs. There was no nerves anymore, just calm breathing. The door opened, and my doctor for the past twenty-one years walked in—Dr. Peterson. He sat down, opened his file, my jaw dropped as if to say something but I didn't, I just sat there, he looked up at me with his long brown eyes and said those words, "I'm sorry to tell you this, William, but you have cancer." I asked if it was bad and he nodded a yes. I took a deep breath as a tear fell from my eyes; something just drained, my hope or age, I never knew something, just plainly left in that moment. I sat there breathing deeper and deeper, just telling myself I can take it, I'm a man, this is nothing; but I knew it was much more than nothing—this nothing had taken my father three years earlier. Dr. Peterson just drew a blank and sat there with me, no words just silence; fifteen minutes had passed. I stood up, looked at him, and said I need some time to go and think things through, really though I just needed time to figure out how to tell my mother who was just sitting there, waiting, more nervous than I ever was. She raised me, she watched me grow, and to find out that her eldest son of four may not outlive her is just, I dunno—it's overwhelming and painful and I'm mixed up and I need a smoke to clear my head, the one thing that gave me this awful lung-filling disease. I walked out of the room and back into the lounge; I walked right up to her and looked at her for a long time. She knew, she felt my pain through those doors; she dropped down and fell to tears. I just stood in awe of this one time, trying so hard not to let it all out.

I don't want him to die though—William, that is—I want a statement of a life flipped upside down and I want him to fight and find love and grow into someone that feels real. He is young, yes, but he will be brave. What is bravery in this world of timeless classics that once were new? Is it really just about fear, or in some distinct manner is it a voice inside telling us to face the words of others to face something more than we ever thought we could, not just fears but life and everything that revolves around life? We were on the second round of our game, knocking down the puppet kids when Andrew's cell rang. "Hey, okay, okay, what why now . . . yea, I guess so . . . 'kay, bye." Andrew then told us how he had a wrestling match the next day and his mom wanted him to get his sleep so we persisted and sat for a bit and then without any haste words toward stopping the fun that we were having, we left, no hard feelings toward Harsh boy, aka Andrew, it was just time to go and so we did, the gusting speed back home through the binds and curves of the road through the shadows of the moon, the light of the stars, and the darkest spots along the ridges of Shuswap Lake. In no time at all, we were back in reaching distance of home; just the other day I found myself in a reassuring moment, one of flaws and scrapes one conceived without knowing where, where was. But I knew I was happy, I knew I was with her—Shelby, that is. Just lying down atop the pitcher's mound, gazing down on us were the stars; we found the Big Dipper but not the little one. She calls it the Tiny Dipper, haha, so cute and so beautiful. Lying there, hands gripped in place, a shooting star hovered by. "Omg, did you see it?" "Yea, haha, I saw it, but did you make a wish, Shelby?" "Aw no, I forgot." Haha, aww, she's so cute with the randomness thing and it just intertwines my heart's depths and gives me a smile worth showing off. "So what did you wish for?" "I wished for a kiss, Shelby." This was a moment, a great one—our first kiss and her very first kiss. I was so lucky for it too; she was a little shy about it, but it was perfect when it all dawned on me. That captivating moment when you wonder for so long if you could last a long time or if you could make it over a year or even a summer so fast when you want it to be so slow, to have fun making, no wasted time or mistakes. In this moment, I wanted a picture-perfect ending with her. Arriving now after dropping Harsh off, we pull into Mitch's driveway, get out with a buzz, and go to the basement. We enter the cooler hollows of his dimmed bedroom, a darker room consisting of a bed and a TV, hardwood-paneled flooring and a whisper of a room aged in doormat fear. I didn't stay here long Al had left an hour ago and I there sitting just talking about life with an honest friend who's words find ways to give me hope. A blink and a stutter the buzz was very much still there I found myself walking the road so unaware that I had left and gone; I'm often like this after a good drinking night, I like walking the road, the silence no longer just a myth it's real it's so pure in the ear that you wonder if someone should pinch you. My friends always ask if I would rather live in Sicamous and my answer is always simply stated as a no and the reason is silence and peace in a country sweet, it's like an eye candy this town, the adventure and the containment, I like It, the independence that is. I remember when Mitch and I wondered after having a few, we ended up at the train crossing, watching those red flashing lights with a buzz, such good entertainment to a lost boy. Four in the morning or so, my morning walk home such grace on a walk with the street lights, the eyes of an empty path home leading me walk in the middle of a paused traffic. If only snow lay down next to its departed ground a look upon thee for everyone to see how farfetched life can truly be. I regret moments in my life time gone, the void so unfilled never will be fill we can't go back not now.

Unproclaimed Words of a Teenage Boy

TIME GONE

Pause; stand still to find what I hide
So confused, so scared; PANIC!
Not wanting to leave, I must
High school, boy, it's over
Look past the handover, the trade
Past for future
I want past but deep down must move on
The start of a new dawn
Memories wanting to last soon will surpass
All good times gone these moments
They didn't ever last long
Later all we'll have is a picture
Emotion killed deeply killed, my childhood is gone;
Goodbye, goodbye.

A monument, a photo—how are we gonna be remembered? Shot in the head, made famous from our death—we're all just history, some past tense that is gone. Don't live in the moment, just simply live without the time, without the clock that makes us count the hours down until we truly are history. I am a boy, I'm weird, average, and I don't care what people think; that's just their weakness. I wake up and go to bed saying this to myself. It's an outlook on my life and I see it as better. This world can be made for everyone; we as humans need to see that, we as humans need to sacrifice. There is joy, there is grief, sadness amongst these, feelings that make us up and break us down. Heart! To scream it is real, a word greater than all, without heart we falter even in a valiant cause. We use it to live, love, we use it for greater emotions felt within; I walk home and lay in my bed. I think of her and sleep well, I wake to a new day, a new beginning, and I leave this place with heart.

9

Silence eluding the misconsumptual boy now; no window in this room, no agonizing, bright streetlight that hallows in demand of an audience. A door half open, half closed sits in refinement of a framed view that copes with still breathing, a creak here and there. His mom wasn't up, the light of the television was not streaming in; pitch-black, only few outlines remaining. There isn't a closet here for that big 2008-year-old boogie man, just a dream catcher for the eighteen-year-old's figurative views of a fucked-up nightmare that holds high hopes of never happening even with the world ending. And that wording of the heart? What heart? I haven't any, just a teen with a word that sums up a great protagonist.

~

I had just woken up thinking of a very lame night of drinking; yes, I had a few and yes, I was hung over, but what's that reoccurring beeping? A note sitting by an unfamiliar alarm clock, the note telling me that my mom was away for meetings. This completely surpassed my memory, her with a week of meetings, meaning with my birthday soon arising: PARTY! In the yard, the whole campout, with the fire and the drunkenness of myself and beloved friends. I gotta plan this shit out, all of it, I want perfection, a masterpiece party in the making. But for now I must be on my way.

It wasn't be a big party. It was fun and I was drunk, but it wasn't big. I had the most important people over, my friends, of course, and that was that; later I would graduate with the graduating class of '08. I'm pretty sure we had the best transport there; it was so elegant in a way like in the movies having three guys walking out of a helicopter wearing their tuxedos, I remember walking past one of the teachers and she said, "Tanner, I thought you were just kidding about landing a helicopter in the back field!" Haha, I just laughed it all off. Grad went well, some great memories. I ACTUALLY FUCKING GRADUATED and that's all that mattered to me. Little time would pass and I would lose interest in that once-amazing girl, deciding I should just go out alone but I do think of someone, someone just below the border. She still lingers, an amazing girl that I still must see. Maybe write a letter, I don't know her number, come to think of it, I don't know much about her but she made me feel, made me feel so real with her laugh and her personality. I don't know, maybe I'm just seeing what I dream; but if she's anything like my dreams, then, well, she's what makes me tick. All those thoughts of a perfect world and her face is the only one I see, but for now she is lost and I wait with one promise at hand I made just to wait to see what light can be given and to go from there. I just hope at the end of that light I find her there bearing down to love, only not for months; yet forever when time is ready to render such a treasure.

~

No, you won't go down alone, soft words in a soft song, revealing so many things now is a hard-pressed heart with almost too many thoughts moving indirectly. But that's okay, it's all natural, all secure to my imagination to my fulfilling standards. Grad has been over now for some time, almost a month, and in time it had showered clear pure rain the brightest views of clarity are seen through my eyes when it rains. Just picture it, soft falling rain over pastures of green and mountains of blue, the beauty of weather, the solitude of nothing, so fining in its bittersweet moments. The river has risen much now; I have heard of mudslides and accidents, lightning showers, and fires all caused and put out by rain.

~

I still remain working with my second family at the grocery store; soon though, I fear I will break. I can't face that job day after day with nothing but a solemn droll face and dreams of greatness being pushed way toward in; it is painful to grad and not move, to stand so still and looking back on it and all you see it all like you were just there, but you can go back and you blow down to a tear of past with no thoughts of what you could ever do with your future, it hurts and it is so remorseful to the soul. Sure, people just tell me to go with it but they don't know. They're not there and they sure as hell aren't me. I just want refinement, I want joy so soon in such a perfect place, but I don't know where and I don't know when nor how. I am just a boy awaiting his demand on some near scene. Smock on, cutter in hand, I stock the shelves, it's not what I want out of life, but it will get me there. I know this from others before me with the terms of hard work and paying off by doing so. Have you ever felt so compelled to help yourself but cannot? A summer of meaningless drinking and for what? 'Cause the small-town scene bores the hell out of you! I'm a joke, I know, but that's okay. I just need to control it all and finish it all and the confidence that eludes my ever-ending lifestyle of not trying or being afraid of the greatest chances, it's those days when giving up and settling for less. Not striving for first, but second best, just flat out hiding when I know! When I know I can be better.

Some days I find it hard to imagine how I fit in, in such a place of dark judgment on others, how I survived grade 8 and 9 growing into a more likeable person year after year. I always thought I would fail trying to fit in, but after grade 9, I just stopped caring what others thought, what others cared for 'cause in the end it's just you, not the emocity of a well-rounded student body. Sure, you make friends, but the staff is teaching you to find a world for yourself on your own to be stronger, independent. And maybe, not maybe it's about teamwork but yet is that not just what a sport is for, or yet again they just teach our history, our literature, and our subtle use of ill-used words such as *fuck* and *asshole* the words of badgering. Just thoughts, pointless rambling thoughts of what school is and was but who knows years from now we may not need education, just machines to shape a world of in fragments.

I mount my placement to the grocery store floor asking directions from managers nothing the sort alike but none of this matters; it never will. If I could keep pace with anything like they do, I would be a great asset to the store, haha, but I'm afraid that will never happen at Askews. I won't lie, I rarely work hard there, if I worked hard I wouldn't enjoy it but I do very much enjoy it with the gang, always very accessible to some great form of humor, between Wayne's antics about my brother's misdemeaning sayings, Mike's great tips of always wearing a condom and Peter's attempts to get everyone in the store soaked in water. They're not your everyday managers, they may be the people that give you orders but at the end of the day you can all go have a beer and bullshit over some stupid article in the paper. My shadow mocks the wall as I sit on my coffee waiting aimlessly to return to the throne of the stock boy. Perched out looking to the floor, I sit upstairs thinking only of home time and when this time will arrive. Work has gone by slow today, not always it does this but some few times it does. Though I must be on my way, coffee has struck the time of up.

~

I saw a paper article the other day, with the thoughts of the world's state and where it will be in the near and distant future, I didn't care. The world will end one day, we can't stop that so we worry and we stress and we have a heart attack because we worry about these animosities that haha unfortunately don't matter just as the Beatles said, "Let it Be." Have you ever been confined to a space, a moment where you felt so weak, the days just slipped away and you losing yourself in dismay. Where the clock went so fast that the happiness once felt wasn't around to last, the dew of the flowers faded, the mentions of your name wiped away. What happened to it all, our lives, our world, we've become so deceptive that we can't see that we're killing ourself as a planet off. My point in this ramble of a thought is that we cannot define a world, we cannot change everyone so why try when the future is the stepping stone of the reaper.

10

Don't try to argue with the facts, embrace this misdemeanor of time with what might be a very great one—the first African American president and already threats on his life, not because he's the president yet because he's colored. So in accordance with the past, what's changed, why is there such a vindication of color in the world, what's the difference when the sun goes down and there're no lights around, we are the same; yet why judge.

What will be? Is that not a question without answer? Some locked door without the Keep Out sign, so we push and push yet nothing happens, no answers just shorter words for that of the same question. Why do we explore, to conquer? Why do we experiment with what was always fine to begin with, I would much rather live than die in some prolonged science experiment. Some days, however, I wish I knew all the answers, yet I think more and see that that would just take the fun out of finding out for myself, like how I die or how the world ends, both very cynical questions yet they break our mind with wonder. Out to the parking lot, to my parents' 2001 F150 Ford, I have now been driving the truck for some time after losing my car and almost my life in a moose-hitting incident. It changed everything you know, every glaze of a shadow moving now I slow, and bittersweet I find no calm movement in this, just a flaw in my heart's content. But what does it all mean? Was it some insignificant warning about a moose? Or was it much more. Is this some lesson to change who I am and what I do with the time that I have on this earth? It all got me captured my thoughts at night, and during the day, it had slowed down my days of thought so much in fact that I had lost a day just thinking of myself and what could change. What if that moose came through the window, would I be done for or paralyzed, never able to perform as normal? This thought is such an understatement on everything.

Out of the parking lot now, I am making a pace slower than an older lady I was once taught before my incident. Though this is all fine to me, it's okay knowing that I'll be safe for the night's drive toward home. I don't get it, do I ever move in the right direction looking for what makes me tick, trying new things to fill a gap that I've never had? I'm lost and I don't know if I'll ever be found, haha, but I do know that someone out there maybe waiting, maybe not, but that's fine if they're not 'cause I don't care. I'd rather just be happy with what I have than be miserable with something much lesser to my heart. I'm gonna find myself one day and through the malice one day I'll just walk away, not caring what the world thinks, just being who I was born to be: great . . . No no, who am I kidding. I'm not great, I'm just a boy who wants to change the world.